BEVERAGE BIZ

is

SHOW BIZ!

ABOUT THE EDITOR

Mary J. Stipe is a freelance writer and editor who lives in Northport, New York. As Managing Editor of *Distinction Magazine: Elegant Living on Long Island,* she has worked with Dave Steadman whose "Spirits" column is a regular feature of the bi-monthly Times-Mirror publication. Their collaboration led to the project of editing this book. As a writer, she specializes in interior design, decorating, gardening, fashion, textiles and crafts. When not at work with words, she enjoys dining out and, of course, a glass of fine wine.

ABOUT THE DESIGNER

Valerie Hnatik is a graphic designer who lives in Lindenhurst, New York. As Art Director of *Distinction Magazine: Elegant Living on Long Island,* she developed the style and image of the publication and continues to design each issue. *Beverage Biz is Show Biz!* reflects her considerable design talent and vision. When not at work on her computer, she too enjoys sampling the fare at area restaurants and checking out the wine lists.

ABOUT THE COVER

Special thanks to Libbey Inc. for use of the cover photograph. The glassware shown is from the Z-Stem by Libbey Collection.

BEVERAGE BIZ
is
SHOW BIZ!

How to Increase Your Restaurant's Bottom Line

by

Dave Steadman

Author of
Restaurant Biz is Show Biz!

Spirited Living Publishing

Beverage Biz is Show Biz!

Published by
Spirited Living Publishing
38 Broadway
Greenlawn, NY 11740
Tel: (631) 862-0240

Library of Congress Catalog Card Number: 99-91344
ISBN 0-9675075-0-2

Dedicated to
Jane E. Schreiber

ACKNOWLEDGEMENTS

Thank you to all of the people you will meet in the following pages who willingly shared their knowledge of the restaurant business for the benefit of you, their peers.

And appreciation to my family, friends and acquaintances who made important contributions to the completion of this book, often without knowing it: Miro Anaya, Paula Bauer, Irwin Bedell, Michael Booker, Dan Cajigas, Ann Camardese, Bob Camillone, Dave Dronkers, Fadi El Baba, Lee Feldstein, Bill Fermoile, Jean Fermoile, George Giokas, Chuck Giometti, Patrice Golde, Joe Goss, Matt Green, Cecilia Jackson, Joe Kelly, Maxine Kilgallon, Frank Lepera, Ray Lepera, Arthur Lewis Jr., Karleen Lewis, Mary Lewis, Matty Lewis, Mark Marcon, "Hundred Thou" Malloy, Jack Mulderrig, Dick Reumann, Raffaela Schaffer, Susan Schreiber, Ted Schreiber, Mitch Shapiro, David Steadman III, Edna Steadman, Kathleen Steadman, Louis Steadman, Marguerite Steadman, Marty Steadman, Michael Steadman and Peggy Steadman.

Contents

BEVERAGE BIZ is SHOW BIZ!

INTRODUCTION 11

PART ONE

1. Mister Show Biz 14
   Jeff Ruby, The Waterfront, *Covington, Kentucky*
   Jeff Ruby's, *Cincinnati, Ohio*

2. That's Entertainment 19
   Henry Schielein, Balboa Bay Club, *Newport Beach, California*

3. Relax, Life is a Long Weekend 22
   Tony Margolis, Tommy Bahama's Tropical Cafe, *Naples, Florida*

4. A Tropical Paradise on the Mainland 26
   Kern Mattei, Mai-Kai Restaurant, *Fort Lauderdale, Florida*

5. Special Welcome for Travelers 31
   Edwin Rios, Chicago Hilton and Towers, *Chicago, Illinois*

6. Fun Food . . . Fun Drinks . . . Fun Attitude 34
   Scott Smith, McCormick & Schmick's, *El Segundo, California*

7. Celebrity Status 36
   Felix Albano, Fiftyseven Fiftyseven, *New York, New York*

PART TWO

8. The King of Grappas 41
Giovanni Francescotti, Giovanni Ristorante, *New York, New York*

9. Celebrate With Your Guests 44
Gillis Poll, Bryant & Cooper Steak House, *Roslyn, New York*

10. Cruising at the Pier 46
Neil Wallace, Queen Mary, *Long Beach, California*

11. Don't Rest on Your Laurels 49
David Laxer, Bern's Steak House, *Tampa, Florida*

12. Raw Bar Draws a Crowd 52
Mark Gambuzza, Ashes Steak House & Seafood Raw Bar
Red Bank, New Jersey

13. Take a Fresh Look at Your Beverage Program 55
Andrea Immer, Starwood Hotels

PART THREE

14. A Lounge Menu Built Around Caviar 60
Erik Blauberg, "21" Club, *New York, New York*

15. It's All About Image 63
Brian Matzkow, Soho Grand Hotel, *New York, New York*

16. Tequila is More Than Margaritas 65
Nelson Portela, The Alamo, *New York, New York*

17. New York's "Authentic" British Pub 70
Deven Black, North Star Pub, *New York, New York*

18. The Microbrewery Challenge 76
Don and Kevin Sullivan, Southampton Publick House
Southampton, New York

PART FOUR

19. Hospitality Plus 83
Monte Silva, Wolfgang Puck Cafe, *El Segundo, California*

20. Where Margaritas Drive the Bar Business 85
Walter Carillo, Cozymel's, *El Segundo, California*
Phil Barragato, Cozymel's, *Westbury, New York*

21. Beach Party 89
Craig Mitchell, Hennessey's Tavern, *Hermosa Beach, California*

22. Live Entertainment Packs 'Em In 91
Paul Hennessey, Lighthouse Cafe, *Hermosa Beach, California*

23. Snug as an Irish Pub 92
Chris Martin and Rory Connolly, The Irish Bank
San Francisco, California and New York, New York

PART FIVE

24. The daVinci of Drink 96
Dale DeGroff, The Blackbird Bar & Restaurant, *New York, New York*

25. It Takes a Flair 100
Scott Young, Bar Smart, *Vancouver, British Columbia*

26. Creating Room Energy 104
Blake Donaldson, Michi Restaurant & Bar, *Manhattan Beach, California*

27. Bartenders are a Rare Resource 107
Michael Waterhouse, Dylan's, *New York, New York*

28. Performance Bartending 109
Vance Campbell, The Roxy, *Vancouver, British Columbia*

29. Tempt Your Guests with a Pre-Taste 112
Kevin Carrigan, Angelo & Maxie's Steak House, *New York, New York*

30. Turning Slow Times into Show Times — It's Magic! 115
Louis Melamed, Tricks on Tap, *Mahtomedi, Minnesota*

PART SIX

31. Zraly on Wine 120
Kevin Zraly, Windows on the World Wine School, *New Paltz, New York*

32. Fine Wine . . . Without Limit 124
Mike McCann, Cité, *New York, New York*

33. Building a Wine Cellar 126
Brian Arbesfeld and Leonard LoRusso, Focaccia Grill, *Wantagh, New York*

34. A Wealth of Fine Wine 129
Gil Travalin, The Carltun, *East Meadow, New York*

35. London was Never Like This! 132
Les Barnes, London Lennie's, *Rego Park, New York*

36. Winning Combinations 138
Carole White, Farfalla Trattoria, *Tinley Park, Illinois*

37. Wine Selection Made Easy 141
Sharon and Peter Cooper, The Harvest, *Pomfret, Connecticut*

PART SEVEN

38. Exceeding Customers' Expectations 146
Drew Nieporent and Michael Bonadies,
Myriad Restaurant Group, *New York, New York*

39. *The* Place for Italian Wines 154
Steve DePietro, Il Cigno, *Scarsdale, New York*

40. Half Bottles to the Rescue 157
Dan Marcheano, The Arches, *Newport Beach, California*

41. Pizza and . . . Wine? 159
Mike Amidzich, Pizza Man, *Milwaukee, Wisconsin*

42. Wine Tastings Generate Dinner Business 161
Sukie Honeycutt, Terra, *Naples, Florida*

43. Wine Flights of Fancy 163
Cloyde Pate, Cork's, *Naples, Florida*

PART EIGHT

44. It's Time for Creative Non-Alcohol Drinks 166
Joe Fassler, ProDine, Inc.

45. Don't Leave Money on the Table 168
Robert Plotkin, Barmedia

46. Go With The Coffee Flow 173
Nick Castronova, The Lamplighter, *Rochester, New York*

47. New York's Coolest Pleasures 175
Ira Freehof, Comfort Diners, *New York, New York*

PART NINE

Dave Steadman's Restaurant Scene 179
Index to Restaurants and Services 185
Index to People 189

INTRODUCTION

Your restaurant is the stage on which you and your staff perform. The stage design and scenery, or lack of it, set a mood. But just as in the theater, success or failure depends on the strength of the script (read food and beverages), the skills of the director and the performance of the actors.

For over a year I have visited restaurants around the country, talking to operators, bartenders, sommeliers, servers, customers and suppliers. I've read what restaurant reviewers and wine writers have had to say. Much of what I've heard is in these pages.

"Restaurants are no longer in the business of just serving food and beverages . . . I am not in the drink business, I am in the entertainment business . . . Fine dining requires fine wine . . . I had to do something different to grow the business . . . The key to us is staff training . . . Today's young servers are confused about their role in selling and serving alcohol beverages . . . People come to The Roxy for entertainment . . . We have entered a new age of celebrity bartending . . . It's the *Cheers* syndrome that drives today's bar business . . . Not every member of a social or business group wants an alcohol drink . . . If you are still thinking that you're in the alcohol business, you're leaving money on the table . . . We are determined that each and every customer finds his or her expectations exceeded . . . It's a tribute to an operating philosophy that shares profits with employees whose commitment to demanding standards ensures our success."

In one form or another, this is what I heard and you will read on the following pages. You'll notice that not everybody is taking the same tack. This is not a cookie-cutter business. Two units of the same chain will do some things differently, while adhering to the basic footprint of the parent. One idea might work for one operator and the exact opposite may do the trick for another. But some refrains are constant:

- You must deliver perceived value to your guests.
- You must treat your employees fairly and with concern.
- You must train your staff, again and again and again.

- You must be innovative and offer your guests what they can't find anyplace else.
- By the time a competitor copies you, you must be three steps ahead.

That's a lot of "musts." You can ignore them — if you don't plan to stay in business for very long.

Another very important "must" is wine. It's not going away. It's a very important part of the dining experience for many of your guests and if you don't deliver what they're looking for, some other restaurateur will. Not everybody wants to order a full bottle, nor does the knowledgeable wine drinker want a glass of no-name red, white or blush wine. A large variety of half bottles is one answer. Offering most of the wines on your list, if not all of them, by the glass is another.

Some of the operators I spoke to found that Private Preserve, a canister that dispenses inert gases into an opened wine bottle, minimized losses due to spoilage, when properly used by staff. This might also work for you. Proper pricing can also ensure that you will not lose money on any bottle that you open.

What is proper pricing for the bottles on your wine list? Some wine writers are telling their readers that restaurants charge too much for wine and point to dramatically different prices among restaurants for an identical wine. The truth is that many restaurateurs do overprice their wines. But there is no simple formula for pricing your wines. Talk with knowledgeable supplier representatives and listen to their advice. Open a dialogue with your wine-drinking guests. Ask them what wines they would like you to carry and let them know what you are doing to ensure a fine wine experience for them, such as maintaining a temperature-controlled wine cellar and/or traveling to wine-producing areas to seek out special wines for your list.

In the next 47 chapters, you will learn how other successful operators have turned challenges into opportunities.

Part One

I am not in the drink business. I am in the entertainment business.
— Jeff Ruby

Restaurants are no longer in the business of just serving food and beverages; we are in the business of offering our guests an outstanding experience when they walk through our doors. And this experience often includes the savoring of fine wines and spirits paired with appropriate foods, along with good entertainment and ambiance.
— Henry Schielein

I remember when apparel retailers put P. T. Barnum to shame. The best showmen today are in the restaurant business, and I find it very exciting to be part of this restaurant world.
— Tony Margolis

If we create excitement among the staff, they will create excitement among our guests.
— Edwin Rios

Mister Show Biz

1

"THE WATERFRONT probably sells more drinks than any place in Greater Cincinnati, but I am not in the drink business," says Jeff Ruby, owner of the restaurant/bar complex on the Ohio River. "I am in the entertainment business."

Inspired by the Al Pacino movie, *Scarface,* which was filmed in Miami Beach, Ruby and associates visited Miami, Maui, Acapulco — wherever in the world he heard there were striking design elements or food and drink offerings.

In October 1986 Ruby opened The Waterfront, built on a barge on the Ohio River. It featured a two-level restaurant, Windows On The Water, with a stairway designed to evoke oohs and aahs from devoted fans of *Gone With The Wind.* The Waterfront was anchored at Covington, Kentucky, with a dazzling view of the Cincinnati skyline.

On a raised platform behind the bar was a white grand piano. "Music has always been an integral part of my restaurants," says Ruby. "It has to fit the mood and it should fit the food. When we serve you lobster with Cuban touches, you may hear Latino music. When I heard *In The Mood* done in a Latino style, I searched for quite a while before finding the CD, a medley of big band numbers played to a Latin beat. It's now part of our mix.

"Inspiration for *Lobster Erpenbeck* came from a dish served at the restaurant in the Hilton in Key West. We flew to Key Largo just to taste that one dish. I flew my chef to Miami to taste a great salad I liked at The Forge, which inspired our *South Beach Bleu Salad.*"

On the Waterfront's opening night, diners were greeted by 11 captains from 11 different countries.

Fun and Frolic, Too

Coconut Joe's, a fun bar offering casual foods, opened at the same time on a small barge anchored next to the restaurant, but with a separate entrance. Inspired by the Fontainebleau, Ruby's designer transformed a river barge in Kentucky into a tropical destination. A rock formation with two waterfalls, a swimming pool, palm trees brought in from Florida every spring and Tiki torches became the setting for the small beach bar serving tropical drinks and beer specials. It was an immediate siren call for the college and post-college crowd.

Hot bands keep the energy level high and 22 club hosts ensure the crowd's exuberance doesn't exceed proper limits. Hosts are the first to greet guests and the last to see them off. Their credo is: "Don't hassle. Don't hustle. Don't muscle."

"Our business is hospitality, not exclusivity," Ruby stresses. "On College Nights we welcome men and women 19 years old and older, with a discount off the cover charge with college ID. Those under 21 wear tags and can only drink sodas or water. Our club hosts pay particular attention to this."

Time to Expand - 1

After the second summer of outstanding business at Coconut Joe's, Ruby bought a larger barge to be tied to the original Coconut Joe's barge. Impressed by the waterfalls in the Hyatt Hotel in Maui, he tracked down the person who designed and built them and hired him to build a waterfall on the new barge. Guests can walk behind it and imagine they're in the tropics.

After spending $1,400,000 on an outdoor restaurant/bar that would be open for only three months a year (late May to Labor Day), Ruby had to get massive publicity to attract the crowds necessary to fill the 1,200-capacity operation.

"Announcing a newly expanded Coconut Joe's would get some press but not the excitement that a new extravaganza would draw," he says. "We went for a name change to Las Brisas and announced a brand new restaurant at a dazzling preopening party for the media, local business people, government leaders, friends and celebrities, many of whom flew in just to attend."

It worked. The headline in the next day's *Cincinnati Enquirer* read: "Viva Las Brisas!" Coconut Joe's remained open with its emphasis on activities for the younger crowd while Las Brisas is promoted to the 28 years and older group. Many diners at Windows on the Water visited Las Brisas and Coconut Joe's after dinner. There is no separation between the two casual tropical concepts — people flow as they will, soaking up the allure of the islands.

Time to Expand - 2

"After 12 years in business, it was time for major refurbishing of the restaurant to reflect what's happening today," Ruby says. "I approached my best customers and offered each of them a $20,000 food and beverage credit, plus special perks, for an immediate payment of $15,000. Some investors are money-hungry; ours were just hungry. We paid them back with food and drink."

This customer financing raised $430,000. Perks included having private use of one of the 11 humidors sunk into the bar top, or one of the "personal wine cabinet spaces" flanking the dining room. Each contributor was also told what object his or her contribution bought. They were treated like partners.

Ruby reopened the restaurant, now named The South Beach Grill, with a 50th birthday party for himself in April 1998, inviting 450 friends to see the new restaurant for the first time. Again, celebrities and sports stars flew in to join with local personalities and media representatives in celebration.

Media coverage was huge and it seemed as if everybody from miles around just had to visit to see for themselves.

Time to Expand - 3

When a downtown Cincinnati restaurant closed its doors in 1999, Ruby decided to open a steakhouse at the site. Noted restaurant and nightclub designer Dave Stevens, of Las Vegas, drew up 14 pages of blueprints and a rendering of the new restaurant.

Completely clearing the old restaurant, Chef Jimmy Gibson set up serving stations for sushi, lamb chops, crab cakes and other finger foods. Well-stocked bars were placed around the restaurant shell. Stevens' blueprints and rendering were placed on the walls and a blaring band greeted 475 people who showed up to celebrate Ruby's 51st birthday.

"We had a blast that made the front page of the next day's papers," Ruby remembers. "Everybody was asked to vote for the new name. When we pulled the ballots out of the box, the choice was overwhelming to call it Jeff Ruby's." Not Jeff Ruby's Steakhouse or Chophouse, just plain Jeff Ruby's. "I'm glad it came out that way," he says, "because 'steakhouse' or 'chophouse' might scare off lunch customers who prefer something light. We take a fun approach to lunch and a serious approach to dinner."

Customer financing provided $500,000 towards renovation costs. This time a $20,000 contribution garnered a $25,000 food and beverage credit, plus perks similar to those that contributors to the South Beach renovation fund received.

With this restaurant Ruby is taking a journey down his personal Memory Lane. He was 13 when he started working in his mother's restaurant, and made many stops before opening the Waterfront complex in 1986. Along the way he learned how to make lemonade out of a lemon, as all successful restaurateurs must.

In 1975, when a Cincinnati lounge he was managing was ordered to shut down for a week because a bartender served a minor, he threw a "Going to Jail" party on the night before the shutdown week. On reopening, he held a "Coming Home" party with a band repeatedly playing songs like: *Done My Time* and *Tie A Yellow Ribbon*. "We did more business on those two nights than we did in a regular week," he remembers. That experience reinforced the importance of fun in building a strong base of regulars.

In his early days Ruby was often called the Toots Shor of Cincinnati, so it's no surprise that the Toots Shor Room is a restaurant within the new restaurant, closed off to accommodate cigar smokers. State-of-the-art ventilation minimizes second-hand smoke for the 60 guests that can be seated at tables and at the bar. Ruby's fond memories of sides of beef hanging in the windows of Gallagher's Restaurant in New York City are also now part of Jeff Ruby's, opened to the public on September 27, 1999.

In preparation for the grand opening, Ruby held a fund-raiser for the Boomer Esiason Foundation fighting cystic fibrosis. Baseball legends Johnny Bench and Pete Rose were among many star athletes attending this $250-per-person event with all proceeds going to the charity.

The day before the grand opening, Ruby hit three home runs. The Sunday *Cincinnati Enquirer* ran a page one profile of his life. His yet-to-be-opened restaurant hosted a campaign fund-raiser for mayoral candidate Phil Heimlich. (Yes, it was the candidate's father who pioneered the maneuver that has saved the lives of more than one restaurant diner.) The third home run? Word quickly circulated that Mark McGuire and five of his teammates had dinner in Jeff Ruby's Wine Cellar that same night — in between two games in which McGuire connected for home runs. Should Jeff Ruby's steaks be investigated?

"Opening night we were bombarded with requests for reservations but only accepted 125, gradually increasing each night until we felt comfortable that our staff could effortlessly handle the 400 or more now filling our seats on busy nights," says Ruby. "Our check average is $71 and our dollar wine sales are equaling our entrée sales. We're happy.

"Running a successful restaurant or bar is no big thing," adds Ruby. "It's hundreds of little things. The key is to create the feeling that people are going into someone's home when they enter that restaurant."

That's Entertainment

"TO BUILD our beverage business, we offer fun food at reasonable prices in our Shell Bar and on The Deck," says Henry Schielein, president of the Balboa Bay Club in Newport Beach, California since 1995.

Taco Tuesdays offer Mexican food at $5 per plate and Margarita specials. Member Mixers feature the Mike McCaffrey Trio entertaining with music from the '30s, '40s and '50s. The promotional flyer states: "If you like Cole Porter and Duke Ellington, you'll love the Mike McCaffrey Trio."

All-you-can-eat-chicken, $9.50 per person, $5.00 for children under 12, is a big draw on Wednesday evenings. Page Cavanaugh's Trio performs and a flyer proclaims: "Don't miss this chance to see the renowned pianist, vocalist and one of jazz music's all-time great performers."

Pasta reigns on Thursday evenings, at $8.50 per plate, and on Fajita Fridays the plates are $7.50. The Fabulous Darvy Traylor Duo takes center stage on Thursday, Friday and Saturday evenings. That ubiquitous flyer again grabs the attention of members with: "People who enjoy Lou Rawls will love Darvy Traylor. From soulful vocals to upbeat melodies to make you feel good, this popular duo will entertain in the Shell Bar for your listening and dancing enjoyment. Traylor sings jazz, blues, swing, ballads, the golden oldies and even country."

And that's just part of what's happening at this 3,000-member private club located about 30 miles south of Los Angeles.

Winemaker Dinners

From September through April, the club holds a monthly Winemaker Dinner in the bay-front dining room, The First Cabin. The chef and featured winemaker mix with the 100 guests and discuss food and wine pairings on the evening's menu.

Since 1995, the dinner series has culminated in The Newport Beach Spring Wine Festival, held at the club over two days at the beginning of May. In 1999, it kicked off with a Friday night Opus One Winemaker Dinner with Gilles De Chambure, senior wine educator for Opus One, discussing the '93, '94 and '95 vintages which were paired with a special dinner prepared by Chef Jean-Pierre Eigenheer and his staff.

Saturday began with a 10:30 a.m. tasting of six premium caviars paired with fine Champagnes and premium vodkas. The main event, "A California Passion," was held that evening. Fifty wineries hosted the walk-around tasting with a buffet of West Coast food specialties. Les Czimber and his jazz trio played throughout the evening.

Each event was priced separately, allowing members to pick and choose their favorites.

Summer Fun

Hamburgers on the beach every Thursday night and frequent concerts are some of the typical summer festivities.

The summer of '99 featured La Primavera Pops Concert with the Irvine (California) Youth Symphony, a 17-piece big-band orchestra under the direction of Bill Strout for dancing under the stars. A Fourth of July bash featured The New Orleaneans, a seven-piece Dixieland band. Throughout the summer, a number of performers were featured including the legendary Four Lads and Lynn Rogers, lead vocalist of the Tommy Dorsey Orchestra, and The Four Freshmen. An Outrigger Canoe Club Beach Party and Luau featured the Notorious Nuckleheads, Polynesian dancers and the '60s band, The Surfaris. A Mexican Fiesta featured José Hernandez and his group of 15 performers, while the Surftones headlined The Last Beach Party of Summer . . . that was outdoors.

On a more formal note — namely white dinner jackets for the gentlemen and evening attire for the ladies — The Governor's Ball heralded summer as Les Brown and The Band of Renown played nostalgic favorites for guests enjoying a superb dinner and memorable wines.

Early August saw the fifth annual Gentlemen's Smoker and Lobster Clambake. (Women are welcome despite the event's name.)

Attendance was limited and, for $250 per person, guests enjoyed superb wines and spirits along with a five-course dinner. A selection of fine cigars, Champagnes, Cognacs, Armagnacs, single malt Scotches, premium bourbons, Ports and liqueurs were on hand, and a band played tropical music to set a "properly decadent tone."

A Cigar Smoker Pioneer

Henry Schielein made headlines in *The Wall Street Journal, The New York Times, Newsweek* and the Boston newspapers when he held a formal cigar smoker at Boston's Ritz Carlton in 1983.

"It was not politically correct at the time," he remembers. "I had just been named general manager of the Ritz and we had a Ladies Tea Lounge that was full for lunch and through the afternoon but was empty in the evening. Since I enjoy a fine cigar myself, I queried our regular patrons and found 75 who also enjoyed smoking a good cigar."

Inviting them to a black-tie cigar smoker featuring a selection of the finest cigars, liquors and wines, accompanied by excellent food, Schielein was pleased to have 50 attend — an amazingly high percentage.

"Some of my staff advised against doing this, fearing an adverse reaction, but just the opposite happened," he adds. "The annual affair now attracts 150 people at $500 a pop for the hotel, and the room remains the Ladies Tea Lounge for lunch and afternoon but now has an evening business as the Cigar Lounge."

When Schielein became general manager of the Ritz Carlton Laguna Niguel in Dana Point, California, he continued the annual cigar smokers, introducing them to The Balboa Bay Club in 1995.

"Restaurants are no longer in the business of just serving food and beverages," says Schielein, "we are in the business of offering our guests an outstanding experience when they walk through our doors. And this experience often includes the savoring of fine wines and spirits paired with appropriate foods, along with good entertainment and ambiance."

Relax, Life is a Long Weekend

WALKING ALONG 3rd Street South in Naples, Florida, you hear the sounds of the tropics and people laughing before you are greeted by a lanai half-filled with people enjoying tropical drinks at well-spaced tables.

It's 11:30 a.m. on a cool Wednesday in January.

Through the palm trees you spot a sign telling you that you have found Tommy Bahama's Tropical Cafe and a banner coaxing you to: "Relax, Life is a Long Weekend."

Who can resist joining in? Not very many, evidently, as business builds through lunch, late lunch and the rest of the day.

Tropical Specialty Drinks are very popular:

Bahama Blast — gold rum, Malibu, raspberry liqueur, mixed with orange juice, pineapple juice and grenadine.

Mai Tai — light rum mixed with lemon and pineapple juice, topped with almond liqueur and a dark rum float.

Hurricane Tommy — light and dark rums mixed with tropical juices, with a dash of lime.

Mango Mimosa — sparkling wine and mango nectar.

Caribbean Bloody Mary — vodka or light rum, tomato juice and island spices.

Baja Margarita — Sauza Conmemorativo tequila, Cointreau and Grand Marnier.

Flavored piña coladas, daiquiris and Margaritas plus other rum concoctions are offered as frozen drinks.

"*Baileys Banana Colada* is the most popular of this group with our tourist guests," says Cyndi Holland, restaurant manager of the Naples operation.

"We combine Baileys and Emmets Irish Creams with fresh banana and Coco Lopez. We top all of our piña coladas with a float of dark rum and we only use fresh fruit and juices in our drinks. Our guests do notice the difference.

"Every drink we serve in our 7-1/2-ounce martini glasses is called a martini," she adds. "And we have fun with the names we give them." Names like: *Dino Martini* — Bombay gin, vermouth and Gorgonzola stuffed olives; *Steve Martini* — Finlandia Vodka, Grand Marnier, orange slice; *Bond, James Bond* — Leyden Gin, Ketel One Vodka, Lillet, lemon twist. Shaken not stirred.

Beer lovers are not ignored. *Tommy Bahama Bungalow Brew* and *Tommy Bahama Bungalow Blonde* are on tap, both made to the restaurant's formulas by Miami Brewing Company. Bottle beers include these plus Kalik Bahamian Brew as well as the standard brands.

With a dinner menu offering mahi mahi, filet of salmon, medallions of pork tenderloin, chicken, ribs, filet mignon and a dozen other items, the wine list is not slighted. Bottle prices range from a $16 cabernet sauvignon to a $55 Veuve Clicquot Brut, as well as over 15 wines offered by the glass.

Who is Tommy Bahama?

He is every man who wants to escape from the drudgery of everyday life to the tropical islands made famous by Hollywood. Or he is the invention of Bob Emfield, Lucio Dalla Gasperina and Tony Margolis, apparel industry veterans who, after extended Florida vacations, would ask themselves: "Why do we have to go back?" Perhaps he is both.

They built a picture of this man, his likes and dislikes, and gave him a name: Tommy Bahama. Together they designed and sourced the kind of clothes Tommy Bahama would wear — fabric light enough for the tropics with a relaxed fit, buttons made from coconut shells. Four months later, in the spring of 1992, the clothing hit the market and quickly caught on.

"We felt that retail sales would really fly if stores would create a tropical setting for displaying our line," says Margolis, "so we discussed opening a company-owned store that would replicate a tropical, thatched roof bar."

From Ready-to-Wear to Restaurant

It wasn't long before the idea blossomed into creating an actual tropical restaurant with an adjacent Tommy Bahama apparel store.

"We knew nothing about running a restaurant but we knew someone who did — Richard D'Amico, a very successful Minneapolis restaurateur," Margolis smiles.

D'Amico couldn't spend full time on the project but he and his partners gave valued advice and flew teams of chefs to Naples, Florida, for two-week stints when Tommy Bahama's Restaurant and Lanai opened in February 1995. Fortunately for all, winter in Minneapolis was D'Amico's slow season.

Operating the Naples concept as the compound manager was Jerry Alajajian, an experienced restaurateur. When he hired Cyndi Holland to manage the Naples restaurant in 1996, he told her, "This is yours. Take care of it; we'll take care of you." She was astonished.

"That had never happened to me before," she says. "That just doubled my determination to do an outstanding job and that became my mantra with my staff. They all responded with an enthusiasm that is picked up by our guests and fed back to us. We're working hard and having fun."

This has also been the mantra for all Tommy Bahamas, and has fueled expansion under the guidance of W. C. Wells as the G-I-C (guy-in-charge), into Sarasota and West Palm Beach in Florida, Palm Desert and Newport Beach in California and Maui in Hawaii. Under consideration for future sites are Coral Gables, San Diego, Hilton Head, Scottsdale and half a dozen other upscale destination resort locations.

"When we opened our first restaurant in Naples, our great concern was that the quality of the food and the attitude of the staff would measure up to the quality of our clothing," Margolis remembers. "The guest experience is our highest priority."

A training program for all employees is centered on the attitude towards guests that "you've come to visit, let's have a good time together."

"Our restaurants cater to an adult couple on vacation who want to have a romantic evening together," says Margolis. "I remember when apparel retailers put P. T. Barnum to shame. The best showmen today are in the restaurant business and I find it very exciting to be part of this restaurant world."

A Tropical Paradise on the Mainland

4

TWO COUPLES are seated in the Mai-Kai Show Room in Fort Lauderdale, Florida, about an hour before show time. They order the *Mystery Drink* for four. A gong is struck every few seconds as a sarong-clad dancer sinuously approaches carrying a huge bowl, which she places in front of one of the gentlemen.

She then performs a seductive hula dance, ending by removing a lei from around her neck and placing it around the guest's neck, kissing him on both cheeks. Regulars will often try to get a smile out of the dancer, invariably without success.

A lot of Mystery Drinks are sold.

Another dramatic presentation is the *Kona Coffee Grog®*. Dark rum, 151 rum, cinnamon sticks, lemon twists and orange peels are put into a ceramic pitcher, flamed and mixed with chopsticks. From a height of two feet, the flaming mixture is poured into a specialty mug partially filled with Kona coffee, honey cream and secret spices. "I want one of those," is immediately heard throughout the dining room. These drinks are show stoppers that consistently draw oohs and aahs.

A Full-Color Drink List

Fifty tropical drinks are shown in full color on the oversized, four-page drink menu — all in distinctive glassware or one-of-a-kind mugs. There are only two exceptions: the *Moonkist Coconut,* served in a hollowed-out coconut, and the *Piña Passion,* served in a hollowed-out pineapple. Guests keep the fruit containers.

The most popular drink is the *Barrel O' Rum.* Made with light rum, dark rum, orange juice, grapefruit juice, syrup and a secret blend of flavorings, it is served in a 32-ounce barrel-shaped mug emblazoned with the restaurant's name. Over 100,000 of these mugs can be found in the homes of Mai-Kai customers.

"With great new flavored rums becoming available, we've extended our 'Barrel' line to include a *Bacardi Limon Barrel* and tropical fruit Barrels O' Rum: the *Banana Barrel* with Cruzan Banana Rum, the *Pineapple Barrel* with Cruzan Pineapple Rum and the *Coconut Barrel* with Cruzan Coconut Rum," says manager Kern Mattei.

Couples are attracted to the *Sidewinder's Fang* served in a collossal 72-ounce snifter, with two 24-inch straws. The zombie is popular with those who respond to the menu's challenge: "Savor slowly this potent potion or you'll cast your lot with the poor souls for whom this drink was named."

New cocktails are continually being created under the direction of head bartender Troy Gallant and then evaluated by Mai-Kai management before being introduced. Appointed in 1993, he is only the fourth head bartender since the restaurant was opened.

One of the newest creations is the *Mai-Kai Rumrunner,* "The Drink You Have Been Waiting For," made with Cruzan Pineapple Rum and Cruzan Banana Rum.

Twelve different rums are necessary to prepare the 50 specialty drinks now offered. These are not cookie-cutter drinks. Each has a very distinctive flavor. The drink list also alerts guests to the strength of each drink by grouping them under these headlines:

Non-Alcohol Tropical Drinks, which include:

Chocolate Typhoon — if you like chocolate and strawberries this is the drink for you.

Maui Sunrise — fresh peach and banana in this tropical drink along with fruit juices and Passion syrup are some of the flavors you will experience.

Mild Tropical Drinks (1-1/4 ounces of spirits) include:

Oh So Deadly® — robust with the rums of the West Indies and the juices of the Tropics.

S.O.S. — a spirituous blend of full-flavored Martinique Rum, tropical juices and West Indies syrups.

Medium Tropical Drinks (2 ounces of spirits) include:

Piña Passion — rums and fruit juices.

Shark Bite® — swim fast and hope for the best. Served with a topping of Appleton 12-year-old rum.

Strong Tropical Drinks (3-1/2 to 4 ounces of spirits) include:

The Barrel O' Rum

Shrunken Skull — dangerous and deadly.

Jet Pilot — fast and courageous, a vigorous blend of heavy-bodied rums and zesty juices.

After Dinner Tropical Drinks include:

Chocolate Snowflake — a cool creamy blend of rums, ice cream, mocha flavors.

Mai-Kai Blizzard — a smoothly blended creation of rum, ice cream and West Indian spices.

Tahitian Coffee — with rum, liqueurs and island spices, topped with whipped cream.

Keeping Up With The Times

"In 1997, after 41 years in business, we expanded our kitchen to allow us to apply classical European culinary techniques to the local flavors of Hawaii," says Mattei. "Our chef offers up to 20 specials marrying French haute cuisine to papaya, mango and macadamia nuts."

Recent specials included: *Pacific Mahi Mahi Over Angel Hair Pasta* — lightly sautéed dolphin topped with a macadamia nut-Boursin cheese stuffing, covered in a roasted-vegetable ginger sauce and served over angel hair pasta — and *Macadamia Nut Encrusted Grouper* — lightly sautéed fresh grouper, served over a vanilla Grand Marnier sauce, topped with dried tropical fruits.

Concurrently, the wine list was expanded to over 200 wines with 15 being offered by the glass. Three or four wine dinners are offered each year in a small dining room seating up to 40 guests. Generally a winemaker will be present to discuss the wines being served.

On a Friday night in November of 1998, the Mai-Kai had a Las Olas Wine Festival Dinner featuring the wines of Dry Creek Vineyards. Winemaker Jeff McBride was present and later wrote Kern Mattei: "The dinner was very, very good and I thought the food pairing was exceptional. Definitely the highlight of my trip. I consider it an honor to have Dry Creek wines associated with the Mai-Kai."

— The Menu —

Reception

Dry Creek Fumé Blanc

Tempura-battered shitake mushrooms with shrimp stuffing

Appetizer

Dry Creek Reserve Chardonnay

Fresh coriander soup

Entrée

Dry Creek Merlot

Oven-roasted beef tenderloin marinated with a Thai pesto
or grilled marinated yellowfin tuna with ginger cilantro butter sauce

Dessert

Dry Creek Chenin Blanc

Mango sorbet served over a honey-roasted pineapple ring
topped with peppered candy cashews

A Change of Pace — Sushi

"Sushi Wednesdays were introduced and have packed the bar from 5 p.m. to 9 p.m. with a different mix of customers," notes Mattei, "generally drinking top shelf brands."

A complimentary sushi buffet offers salmon sushi, tuna sushi, Peking duck roll, boxed salmon sushi, boxed tuna sushi, shrimp sushi, California roll, J. B. roll, Mai-Kai beef roll and tuna roll. Happy hour from 5 to 6:30 p.m. offers the "second drink on the house." Sake and Kirin Japanese beer are also featured.

Cigar Friendly

Mike Bolivar and Mai-Kai Co-owner Dave Levy spent considerable time in the Dominican Republic tasting different tobaccos to develop a unique blend for their D & B Gold Reserve Cigar Collection. These were introduced to Mai-Kai customers in 1998 accompanied by a selection of "sippin' rums," flavorful spirits as smooth as many Cognacs. Bacardi 8, Appleton 12 year Reserve, Ron Barcelo Emperador, Cruzan Estate "Single Barrel" Reserve and Zacapa Centenario Limited Production are some of the more than 40 rums offered. This has been very well received by guests and will be expanded.

How it all Began

Inspired by Trader Vic's and Don the Beachcomber restaurants, Chicagoan Robert Thornton's teenage dream was to someday open a Polynesian restaurant in America — one that would be totally authentic in its decor as well as the food and drink offered.

In 1956, he and his brother, Jack, decided to build this restaurant in Fort Lauderdale, Florida. They built on land far from the center of town, on a two-lane road cutting through scrubby pastureland. The food was authentic and good; the colorful drink menu offered an eye-catching selection of profitable tropical drinks. Waitresses were beautiful; sarongs were skimpy. It was dramatically different from any other Florida restaurant.

Tourists quickly discovered its charms and enough year-round residents were attracted to keep things busy during the off-season. The Thorntons were smart enough to realize the locals were their bread and butter and cultivated their steady patronage. To this day most of the business comes from the local residents.

Five years after opening, the *Islanders' Review* was presented in the 300-seat Show Room. The review, a presentation of the newest dances, songs and costumes of the tropical islands, has been choreographed since 1982 by Mireille Thornton, widow of Robert Thornton and owner of the Mai-Kai. She annually visits Tahiti to keep abreast of what's new, and keep the *Review's* content current.

5 Special Welcome for Travelers

"CONVENTIONEERS keep Chicago's hotels in business. That's a no-brainer," says Edwin Rios, director of food and beverage operations for the Hilton Chicago and Towers. "It's my job to attract them to our restaurants and lounges.

"Long before the convention opens, we sit down with the meeting planners to determine when people will be in the hotel and when events begin, break and end," he continues. "We then make plans to circumvent that walk to the elevator. We want to grab people before they head to other restaurants."

For major conventions meeting at McCormick Place, the shuttle bus drop-off for the hotel is at the entrance to Kitty O'Shea's, an unabashedly Irish pub. As people pour into the hotel, they are greeted outside the pub with samples of Irish beer; the sounds of a band pull many of them into the pub for a full pint. It's fun, and people linger. Others continue on their way, but many stop in later in the evening or week.

If you visited or stayed at the Hilton during the National Restaurant Association Show, you may have heard a three-piece jazz band playing in the lobby as the crowd was flowing in from McCormick Place. Only a few paces away is Buckingham's, a lounge known for its 100-bottle collection of single malt Scotches and wide selection of vintage Port wines. Single distilled Cognacs — Izambard, Camp Romaine and Le Peu — are a new spirit addition.

One evening, a couple in kilts were offering free tastes of some of the Scotches and knowledgeably answering guests' questions. To one side, a gentleman was hand rolling fine cigars which guests could purchase. From 4 p.m. to 8 p.m., happy hour prices prevailed and sushi was served while a pianist played a selection of lively tunes.

At the same time, Lakeside Green, at the hotel's Michigan Avenue entrance, had its own brand of entertainment in full swing with the Michigan Avenue Martini Bar ready with specialty martinis such as *Chicago Fire, Lakeshore Drive Lemon Drop, Lakeside Green Martini, Oak Street Beach* and favorites: *Conrad Cosmopolitan* (vodka, splash of cranberry juice, dash of Cointreau and lime juice, lemon twist) and *Conrad Chocolate Martini* (vodka, Godiva chocolate liqueur and chocolate shavings).

Posters in lobby areas and on elevators promoted these activities as well as nighttime entertainment at the different venues. The daily buffet and smoothie bar at the Pavilion restaurant, as well as breakfast specials at Lakeside Green, were also posted.

The lobby tastings at the entrance to Buckingham's begin at 4 p.m., to attract early arrivals from the convention floor. On the first evening (the night before the convention opened) it was Champagne. The second evening offered a Chilean white wine — Santa Rita. The third evening it was an Australian wine; the fourth evening was a tasting of four Warre's Ports, with a representative of the Port house explaining the why and how of decanting; the fifth evening of the convention was the malt Scotches.

"Of course, our business is much more than conventions," says beverage manager Mike Miller. "We are a regular home away from home for frequent business travelers and celebrities. Leisure visitors to the city also fill a good number of our guestrooms. One reason we are so popular is the reputation our restaurants and bars have established for uniqueness and being fun."

When Kitty O'Shea's Pub was opened in 1986, Midwesterners were amazed to find an authentic-looking Irish pub offering live Irish music and a staff that included Irish men and women, brought over on 18-month visas, who imparted a knowledge about all things Irish to their American counterparts as well as to the pub's guests.

"From day one we promoted Irish whiskey as being more than something to put in coffee," Miller says. "Ireland produces fine aged whiskies along with some Irish single malts. Our guests have come to appreciate them so much that we are now the second largest purchaser of Irish whiskies in the United States."

At the Michigan Avenue Martini Bar, separate from Lakeside Green's main bar, a full-sized cigar humidor is placed next to the bar to accommodate the huge demand for cigars.

Bartenders decide what the bar menu will consist of. An in-demand specialty is the *Martini Salad* — a selection of different lettuces in a pint glass along with a shot of raspberry vinaigrette dressing, shaken and poured onto a salad plate — accompanied by a martini.

"We have a transient clientele, making it imperative that we quickly size up the guest and relate to his or her needs and interests," says Tom Symenski, head bartender at Buckingham's. "Our first priority is to make everybody feel special. For guests intrigued by our huge selection of single malt Scotches (over 100), we will suggest trying a single malt sampler of 3/4-ounce servings of three different malts and we'll discuss the flavors of each. Another time we'll try a different assortment. That guest wants to return when he or she is next in Chicago and gradually he or she becomes quite knowledgeable about malts."

All restaurant staff members are required to attend two four-hour training sessions on Port wines. These are held prior to evening dinner hours. A test is given at completion of these sessions and failure keeps the waiter or waitress off the floor until that person finally passes the test. Whenever new wines or spirits are introduced, every 4 to 6 weeks, experts from the industry address the staff about the products.

"If we create excitement among the staff," says F&B Director Rios, "they will create excitement among our guests."

Fun Food... Fun Drinks... Fun Attitude

6

"SEATING 280, plus another 100 on the outdoor patio, places us among the smaller of the 23 McCormick & Schmick's restaurants," says Scott Smith, GM of the location in El Segundo, California. "Dinner reservations fill up quickly due to our strong relationship with area concierges. We're only ten minutes from LAX and its surrounding hotels. Saturday nights are fully booked by the preceding Tuesday, but we make an effort to seat people within 30 minutes when a concierge calls."

To keep the large cocktail lounge busy, Scott Smith promotes specialty drinks and lighter beers, since many local customers frequent the nearby beach and are health-oriented in their eating and drinking.

That doesn't keep them away from martinis, though. Twelve premium and super premium vodkas grace the back bar, along with Bombay, Beefeater and Tanqueray gins. There's even some vermouth back there.

"People are going where the fun is," Smith says. "We'll occasionally have early evening tastings of exciting spirits products. Recently Miro Anaya and two of her models introduced our guests to Almendrado Tequila, a very tasty almond-flavored tequila. They posed with guests for pictures and everybody in the lounge enjoyed the fun. It helped that the tequila was excellent."

It's Hard Not to Have a Good Time

A special \$1.95 Happy Hour Menu offers Cajun fish tacos with black beans and salsa, chicken wings with Cajun spicy sauce, two-cheese quesadilla with pico de gallo and sour cream, Hama Hama oyster shooters with cocktail sauce, stuffed jalapeño poppers with ranch dressing, New York cheeseburger with french fries, Cajun fried calamari with cocktail sauce, pepperoni and cheese pizza, deep-fried chimichanga with sour cream and Mexican salsa, ground chuck beef chili over fries and bay shrimp cocktail with Tabasco mash and a half loaf of bread (for 95 cents).

The only qualification is a \$2.50 drink purchase.

Fun food . . . fun drinks . . . fun attitude by the staff . . . customers have to try really hard not to have a good time.

"Once a month, on a slow dinner night, we offer winemaker dinners " says Smith. "These always draw well. For continuing wine sales in the dining rooms, we have monthly, hour-long training sessions for our wait staff. This is important because two-thirds of them are not wine-knowledgeable. We'll generally taste and discuss three wines of one varietal, determining how these wines should be presented to our guests and what foods would be appropriate with each of them."

Complementing the in-house promotion is a program of small-business networking. Smith is an active member of the Chambers of Commerce in El Segundo, Manhattan Beach and Redondo Beach. He supports all of their social activities and, in turn, promotes the restaurant's ambience for their personal pleasure as well as for the scheduling of business events, banquets or client entertaining.

"This type of networking builds our events," he says. "To be successful over a period of time, a restaurant must have a solid local customer base."

Since our original interview, Scott Smith was given the responsibility of re-establishing the grandeur of Spenger's Seafood House in Berkeley, California. "It's a timeless, traditional, 110-year-old living antique that McCormick & Schmick's purchased and remodeled," says Smith. "While incorporating some of McCormick & Schmick's signature foods, the menu will reflect the dishes that Spenger's has been famous for."

7 Celebrity Status

FIFTYSEVEN Fiftyseven is arguably the highest dollar volume hotel bar in New York City, perhaps the world. Located in the prestigious Four Seasons Hotel, it's a magnet for The New York Set — savvy people from show biz, Wall Street, the business elite and international travelers.

It's a man's bar, with martinis priced at $14 and a selection of six cigars priced at upwards of $15. An average week will produce $2,000 in cigar sales.

This also attracts many women who want to be with or meet powerful men, creating electricity in the room and interaction among the guests that fosters a sense of festivity. The buzz is energizing and laughter is frequent. On occasion one regular guest, a former opera singer, will burst out in song to the applause of the room.

"The bar scene is like a movie and I'm the director," says Felix Albano, manager of the restaurant bar. "All the actors [clients] have their own scripts and the fun part is in telling everybody where to stay and how to read their lines."

People patiently wait behind a satiny rope to be admitted. Some for 30 minutes or more if they are not guests at the hotel, celebrities or frequent visitors. The best time for the casual visitor to be seated is promptly at 4 p.m., when the room has not yet been filled, and later, between 9 and 10 p.m., when there is a lull.

The ground rules are simple. Hotel guests are the first priority and are immediately admitted to the bar and seated at one of the four tables kept open for unannounced arrivals.

Occasionally a surge of business will see all 27 tables in the room occupied when a hotel guest arrives. He or she will be admitted to the bar and given the next table that opens.

All celebrities are seated as quickly as possible, generally at a table in the back row, against the wall for maximum privacy. Most are guests at the hotel and the others generally call ahead. Regulars from the business community are given the next priority in admittance to the bar.

"When a table opens up, aside from the four that I try to keep available for hotel guests and celebrity drop-ins, it is given to people at the bar who are polite and have been patient," says Albano.

"Those who have been rude or obnoxious will be periodically soothed but will not get a table. I try to chat with people at the bar every fifteen minutes or so, letting them know about possible table openings. They appreciate knowing that I care."

Be Firm but Never Arrogant

People will try to jump the line, producing a variety of excuses when invariably stopped and politely, but firmly, escorted to the back of the waiting line. Others who have been admitted to the bar and then waited and waited and waited for a table to open up for them, occasionally become noisy about countless tables being given to "latecomers." Albano, who listens and nods at their complaints, promising to try to be more accommodating on their next visit, soothes them. When one guest vowed to never return, Albano politely shrugged but later told an associate, "He'll be back." And he was.

"I will not tolerate arrogance, in myself or my staff," he says. "Whether or not I can always give a guest what he or she desires, for whatever reason, that person should always be treated with the utmost respect. This is the cardinal rule of hospitality, be it the elegant Four Seasons Hotel or the down-to-earth Main Street Cafe."

His first position after graduating from University of New Hampshire hotel school was to manage the cafeteria at the New York Hilton. "The best experience possible for working in New York," he states flatly. "I got to personally know the union leaders, the workers and the hotel's managers . . . 'the players.' It was an education you don't get in school and it gave me invaluable insight into what I can expect from my staff and what they expect from me."

Thirteen cognacs are offered, the most expensive being

Courvoisier Erte and Remy Martin Louis XIII; sixteen single malt Scotches, priced from $11 to $30; and six fruit Margaritas, all priced at $16 and carrying an admonition to refrain from requesting salt on the rim "so that you may enjoy all the fresh, lively taste that the fruit in these drinks has to offer." And, of course, martinis, the epitome of what the cocktail scene is all about. These have about as much resemblance to the martinis of the flapper age as the SST has to The Spirit of Saint Louis.

Martini choices range from a traditional gin or vodka martini to a combination peach vodka and peach nectar; vodka, Chambord and pineapple juice; vodka, strawberry liqueur and Champagne. Robin and Mike Meyers tasted many variations before coming up with Stolichnaya Vanil vodka, Malibu rum and pineapple juice — now known as the *Robin and Mike Martini* and one of the best sellers.

A First Class Presentation

Cocktail waitress Susan Blank carries a tray with a traditional martini glass and a stainless steel individual cocktail mixer filled with one of sixteen choices presented to guests. Setting the glass in front of the guest, she fills the glass and returns, when appropriate, to pour the remainder of the drink left in the mixer and ask if he or she would like to reorder.

When Ms. Blank serves a glass of wine, she carries the bottle of wine requested to the table, pours a generous amount into the appropriate wineglass and then returns the bottle to the bar.

Memorable Endings

"After the theater we have many guests for a late snack or dessert, some also ordering a glass of Port wine, a Cognac or single malt Scotch," says Albano. "It's a nice way for guests to finish an evening."

Since this was written, Felix Albano has taken a new position with the management team of Del Frisco's Double Eagle Steak House, opening in NYC early in 2000, on 6th Avenue between 48th and 49th Streets.

Part Two

Wine and spirits are not confined to "a season" any more.
People are more comfortable in themselves and don't
feel that they have to let the outside climate dictate what
they will eat and drink inside our climate-controlled
dining room, bar and upstairs cigar club.
— Mark Gambuzza

We are developing an exciting array of non-alcohol
drinks that will change with the seasons.
Why miss parts of the day when guests don't care for an
alcohol drink — breakfast, lunch and mid-afternoon?
— Andrea Immer

Martinis are so popular that at least twice a month
we are asked to have a separate Martini Bar for catered functions.
— Neil Wallace

Although wine prices have increased in general,
one will still be able to find great wine bargains.
Simply challenge the sommeliers to bring you something
fabulous in the $30-to-$50 range. You will not be disappointed.
— David Laxer

The King of Grappas

IF YOU STILL think of grappa as the raw brandy Italian laborers quickly snorted while flexing their macho images, let me introduce you to Giovanni Francescotti, of Giovanni Ristorante in New York City.

"At one time grappas were quite rough as winemakers squeezed every drop of wine out of the grape before turning the pomace (the remains of the grapes) over to the distillers," says Francescotti. "When grappa sales plunged in the '70s, distillers had to rethink their product. At the same time an increasingly sophisticated wine drinker was demanding better quality wines, forcing winemakers to use first run must and to stop squeezing every drop of wine out of the grapes. The new focus was on producing single variety grappas, using the higher quality pomace of a single type of grape."

By the time Francescotti opened Maruzzella on Manhattan's Upper East Side in 1987, he was able to have an upstairs Grappa Bar featuring 150 high quality grappas — plus 78 single malt Scotches, 70 to 80 Cognacs and Armagnacs and 10 wines by the glass. There were ten tables and room for 12 at the bar to accommodate those who stopped in after having dinner downstairs or, frequently, at nearby restaurants.

Time To Expand

In 1994, Francescotti opened Giovanni Ristorante on 55th street between Fifth and Sixth Avenues in Manhattan. "We present cuisine from the northeastern-most regions of Italy . . . Veneto, Friuli-

Venezia Giulia and Trentino-Alto Adige," he says. "Light tomato sauces, risotto, homemade pastas and lightly cooked seafood. We use very little cream."

The wine list offers 300 wines from all over the world and another 100 wines are aging. When they are considered ready, waiters will suggest them to guests. Ten wines are always offered by the glass.

Thirty wines are listed under the heading: "Great Wines That People Don't Care About."

"These are very good wines, reasonably priced between $20 and $50, that don't receive much publicity," says Francescotti. "Even avid wine drinkers might not know about them, so I draw attention to them."

One hundred very select grappas are offered, over 30 from well-known, single vineyard wines. "My personal single vineyard favorites are the grappas from Sassicaia, Gaja and Ruffino's Gold Label, especially DaPonte made from Prosecco in Veneto, where the best grappas come from," he says. "The classic great grappas are represented by Levi, 'the king of grappas,' and very difficult to get Jacopo Poli and Nonino, bottled in hand-blown glass."

Ruth Reichl, then restaurant reviewer for the *New York Times,* wrote of Giovanni, ". . . an astonishing selection of grappas and a special place to spend an afternoon."

While some spirits are sold at lunch and early afternoon, most people order a glass of wine or bottled mineral water at that time. But come five o'clock and it's martini time. Almost 200 martinis will slide across the bar on most weeknights. Guests desiring spirits after dinner often adjourn to the upstairs Club Room where cigars can also be enjoyed thanks to a state-of-the-art filtering system that continually cleans the air. In an average week guests consume a case of grappa, three to six bottles of Cognac, ten bottles of Port wine, a lesser quantity of various liqueurs and purchase perhaps a hundred cigars.

Private Parties

"Some of our regular customers belong to wine clubs, one of them so new that it doesn't yet have a name," Francescotti adds. "We cooperate with them to produce extraordinary wine and food events for their groups in one of our upstairs rooms. We make no profit on these affairs; it's an opportunity to return something to our regular clientele and give our chefs an opportunity to exercise their creativity. When my wife and I join a festivity, we pay our share of the evening's cost."

One evening, it was a Chateau d'Yquem dinner. Three vintages — 1967, 1988 and 1990 — were served with appetizers of fruit and foie gras sautéed in two different ways. The entrée was a veal chop with a foie gras sauce, accompanied by Maya Dellavalle red wine. Then it was time to return to the d'Yquem.

Another evening, it was a White Truffle Dinner. Over a pound of white truffles were required for the 20 guests. As an appetizer, large ravioli with an egg yolk in each filling were sautéed in butter and topped with Parmesan cheese and slices of truffles. As guests opened the ravioli the egg yolk mixed with the truffles for the ultimate taste sensation. Fettucini and risotto with white truffles, as well as veal chops with white truffles, then followed. This was a lingering evening as guests consumed 20 bottles of red wine, 20 bottles of white wine and over 10 bottles of Port wine. Nobody drove home. Taxicabs and limos saw that everybody got home safely and pleasantly.

9 Celebrate with Your Guests

THE NEW YORK *Times* (April 13, 1997) heralded Bryant & Cooper Steak House of Roslyn, New York, "arguably the best steakhouse on Long Island." With the atmosphere of a private club it has long been a destination for affluent business people.

"Every night, at about 7 p.m., the tables start filling up with business executives and their spouses," says co-owner Gillis Poll. "We are known for the quality of our meat and the skill of our chef with fish and seafood dishes."

After dinner, some guests adjoin to the bar room where smoking is permitted, to light up cigars and enjoy a drink while they talk business. Those who prefer to get away from the cigar smoke, can enjoy a liqueur or a dessert with coffee at the other end of the bar. The restaurant easily sells over 100 Davidoff cigars a week.

The Ultimate Martini

Guests are invited to: "Mix your own ultimate martini." Poll prominently features on his back bar what he considers the "happening" brands. In 1999, these included Absolut, Ketel One, Belvedere, Grey Goose, Chopin, Tanqueray Sterling and Sundsvall, a new, imported vodka from Sweden.

The mixing is actually done by bartender Peter Mooney, after determining how the guest wants the drink prepared and with what ingredients.

Cheering the Dow Jones 10,000

Since many of Bryant & Cooper's customers are stockbrokers, Poll felt a special celebration was in order when the Dow Jones Average broke through the 10,000-point barrier. Accordingly, letters were sent to all local brokerage firms inviting executives and sales staff to a celebratory party from 4 p.m. to 7:30 p.m. on the day the market first surged over 10,000.

When that day came, over 50 people feasted on filet mignon served on a French baguette with a mushroom garlic sauce, smoked Norwegian salmon, super jumbo shrimp, prosciutto-wrapped bread sticks, crudités, whatever they wanted to drink and a Davidoff cigar — all complimentary.

"The purpose of the party was to celebrate our guests' success along with them," says Gillis Poll. "People are still talking about the fun they had and are looking forward to another celebration when the Dow passes 15,000. Actually, we enjoyed it so much that we're going to host a "Halfway to 15,000 Party" when the Dow crosses 12,500."

10

Cruising at the Pier

FOR SHIPWRECK '99, 50,000 people paid $20 each to run the gauntlet of over 200 "monsters" lurking in five terrifying mazes of a haunted ship anchored at Long Beach, California.

This was not just any ship, but the legendary Queen Mary, which once proudly traversed the Atlantic Ocean 1,001 times. On its last voyage the ship continued on to the Pacific and permanently anchored in Long Beach Harbor. As a troop carrier during World War II, the Queen Mary was known as "The Grey Ghost" and, over the years, employees, guests and visiting psychics have reported unexplainable events and paranormal activity. What a place for a month-long celebration of Halloween!

Five blood-curdling, twisted mazes including The Haunted Hull of Horror, the evil Londontowne of Terror, the paralyzing Decks of the Dead, the psychotic Marketplace of Madness and, finally, Factory of Fears, lead guests through five decks to deep below water level. Fortunately, there are portable bars on three decks, as well as the chic Art Deco Observation Bar, The Promenade Cafe, Sir Winston's and Chelsea. There frightened guests can restore their spirits with food and/or drink, ready to once again challenge the mazes or saunter over to the adjacent Queen Mary Exhibit Hall to join the nightly dance party featuring on-air radio personalities from KROQ-106.7, KPWR-Power 106 and 102.7, KIIS-FM.

"Halloween month kicks off our busy season," says Beverage Manager Neil Wallace. "Our 16 function rooms are fully booked at Christmas-party time.

On New Year's Eve we will have eight different parties, each with its own flavor of music including top 40s, big-band, classics, country, jazz, retro '70s disco and hot Latin dance. Our regular bars will be augmented by 50 portable bars to serve drinks and Queen Mary Champagne to over 6,000 celebrants."

Journey Through Time

For the second in a series of historic exhibits, "The Treasures of the Last Russian Emperor" were exhibited aboard the Queen Mary in the summer of 1999. This premier, U. S. exhibit contained 481 priceless artifacts.

The Chelsea Seafood Restaurant offered Temptations from Russia, a choice of five Russian vodkas, Smirnoff Black, Absolut and Ketel One, *Siberian Breeze* made with Smirnoff Black, *Glacier* made with Stoli Limonaya and 7-Up, and a Black Russian.

A Russian Specialty Dinner was also offered with an appetizer choice including three caviars, buckwheat blini with sturgeon caviar and sour cream or a Ukrainskii Borsch. Poached sturgeon with mushroom and crabmeat sauce was the entrée and dessert was apricot sponge cake with lemon butter-cream filling and rum syrup.

Scottish Heritage

Since the Queen Mary was launched at John Brown Shipyard in Clydebank, Scotland, what would be more fitting than hosting a Scottish Festival at the ship?

"Since 1994 we have put on a Scottish Festival in mid-February," says Tim Smith, Observation Bar supervisor. "In the Observation Bar we feature eight single malt Scotches, as well as premium Scotch blends. A variety of Scottish goods are available on the ship and ashore in the Queen's Marketplace alongside the ship. Portable bars on three ship levels are necessary to properly serve the huge turnout."

At other times the Art Deco Observation Bar is kept busy serving martinis. "Martinis are so popular that at least twice a month we are asked to have separate Martini Bars for catered functions," says Wallace.

Two specialty cocktails are particularly popular: *Peachee* — Myers' dark rum, DeKuyper Peachtree Schnapps, pineapple juice and cream of coconut — and *Angel's Reef* — Kahlua, Captain Morgan, Parrot Bay Coconut rum, dark crème de cacao and cream.

The *Designated Driver Drink* also sells well — pineapple juice, orange juice, piña colada mix, blended until it's smooth and creamy.

"While we work very hard at delivering new experiences for our guests, never resting on yesterday's laurels," says Wallace, "there are some traditions that local people insist we continue. One of these is the Queen Mary's Champagne Sunday Brunch, legendary for its 50-plus entrées from around the world. It is served in the original first class dining room, The Grand Salon. Looking around the room at this time, you quickly realize that many guests are not having brunch at a pier in Long Beach, California; they're having brunch in the middle of the Atlantic Ocean on a beautiful sunlit morning."

11 Don't Rest on Your Laurels

WHILE BERN'S Steak House in Tampa, Florida, has not changed its approach to the quality of food served and the high standards bred into its service staff (see "No Detail Is Too Much Trouble," Chapter 16 of *Restaurant Biz Is Show Biz!)*, its beverage service has changed.

"While we still carry 6,500 different wines, the make-up is decidedly heavier in California and other American wines than it was ten years ago," says David Laxer, son of founders Bern and Gert Laxer. "Many are single vineyard and boutique wines not usually found in restaurants not located near their vineyards."

With half bottle choices increasing dramatically, Laxer has trimmed his by-the-glass selections to 175 from 300. Under the watchful eye of Wine Steward Ken Collura, simply recorking an opened bottle of red wine and returning it to the temperature- and humidity-controlled wine cellar, maintains the integrity of the wine for two to three days.

On opening the menu you are immediately greeted with three messages. One tells you about Bern's organic farm that produces the vegetables and salad greens you will be enjoying. Another message tells you why the restaurant is truly unique. The third message talks to you about wine. Here's an excerpt: "We've accumulated the largest variety of wines ever assembled anywhere in the world — not because we want the 'largest' list, but because we want you to be able to select any kind of wine from practically anywhere in the world — from everyday wines you've not had a chance to try, to rare wines you could never locate — all at very fair prices."

Great and rare wines are not inexpensive. Laxer says in a recent newsletter: "Although wine prices have increased in general, one will still be able to find great wine bargains. Simply challenge the sommeliers to bring you something fabulous in the $30-to-$50 range. You will not be disappointed."

Wine Dinners

Four wine dinners a year have been offered over the past few years and this number will increase to seven or eight in 2000. These are generally held during Florida's off-season, attracting about 40 people, and a winemaker or vineyard owner is always present to interact with guests and answer questions about the wines being served.

In February 1999, a dinner was held featuring the wines of Domaine Romanée-Conti, presented by Aubert de Villaine, managing director. "Only two restaurants a year are permitted to host a dinner featuring the wines of Domaine Romanée-Conti, historically the most sought after red wines in the world," says David Laxer. "We tasted all of the red wines the Domaine produces, from the earlier maturing Echézeaux, the aristocratic Grands Echézeaux, Romanée-St. Vivant, Richbourg, La Tache and Romanée-Conti." After a tasting of all the wines from one vintage, dinner was accompanied by older wines from the Domaine. Guests were limited to two people per invitation at the all-inclusive cost of $195 per person.

Annual Winefest

In April 1999, the second annual Winefest was held on the day after the ending of the long-running Sarasota Winefest. "All of the winemakers attending the Sarasota Winefest are happy to stay over another day to participate in our event," says Laxer. "We close our nearby SideBern's restaurant to the public for that Sunday and put a tent over its parking lot.

Over 800 people, paying $25 each, flow in and out of the restaurant and tented area, choosing from 250 wines, a variety of foods and espressos, iced teas and bottled waters. A wine shop allows them to purchase or order bottles of wines that they particularly enjoyed."

Harry Waugh Dessert Room

For coffee, brandy and desserts, diners at Bern's still prefer to adjourn to the upstairs Harry Waugh Dessert Room. Individual nooks, created from the wood of wine casks, create a special ambience for couples to privately toast each other, or groups of three to twelve to have a convivial ending to a meal, without intruding on others.

An attractive 65-page menu lists desserts from Bern's bakery, after-dinner drinks, an expanded selection of vintage Ports and Cognacs, Armagnacs, 160 single-malt Scotches and hundreds of dessert wines by the ounce. Thirteen vintages of Chateau d'Yquem are offered by the bottle; three of them are also offered in one-tenth sizes.

A telephone connects guests to the piano player who gladly plays all requests. It brings to mind the advertising slogan for a New York upscale grocery chain: "If you don't live near a Gristedes, move."

Adding Energy to the Lounge

The lounge was redecorated and brightened in late 1999 to create an energy necessary for cocktail business today. The martini list offers ten varieties of traditional martinis with unique flavors and essences.

A caviar bar invites guests to try 26 caviar varieties in one-ounce servings. Guests are advised that the classic accompaniments for caviar are fine quality, icy-cold vodkas and iced Champagnes.

SideBern's

SideBern's, located two blocks from Bern's Steak House, was created to appeal to a generally younger crowd than the steakhouse attracts. While the menu has two steaks (from the steakhouse aging room), it also offers Caribbean, Fusion and Asian-influenced dishes, with nightly specials.

Over half of all guests are business travelers. Athletes from the local teams, and their fans, also make up a big part of the patronage.

The greats don't stay great by resting on their laurels.

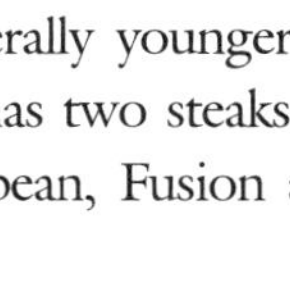

12 Raw Bar Draws A Crowd

OVERSIZED SHRIMP. Fresh oysters and clams waiting to be shucked. Stone crab legs glistening. And caviar . . . chillingly cold from the bed of ice sunk into the bar top. People at the bar can't resist it. Passers-by glancing through the window spot this array and make a quick turn into the bar.

When bartenders ask, "what'll you have," they expect a drink order. At Ashes Steak House & Seafood Raw Bar in Red Bank, New Jersey, it's not unusual for a bartender to hear, "How about some of those shrimp and a half-dozen clams." Then they get a drink order.

"Our *Raw Bar Sampler* is very popular: one pound lobster, three oysters, three clams and three shrimp for $32," says Bar/Beverage Manager Mark Gambuzza. "Frequently, because our seafood sauce is so spicy and strong, people order red wine to drink with our raw bar items. By the glass, merlot is king. When bottles of red are ordered, generally at tables along with dinner, the big call is for cabernet sauvignons and the Super Tuscans."

Ashes, opened on June 30, 1998, as a restaurant and cigar bar, now has 540 dues-paying members of its private cigar club. It attracts an upscale, savvy, well-dressed clientele to its restaurant and bar, with three tables out of four ordering one or more bottles of wine. People are comfortable in their knowledge of wine and are not averse to trying something new at the suggestion of the server. Oversized, 19-ounce long-stemmed wineglasses are filled to about one-third of capacity, for the fullest enjoyment. Guests enjoy swirling the wine and nosing it before taking the first sip.

When the dining room pace is not too hectic, servers will suggest two Port Wine Flights for diners to choose from as an after dinner treat: *Century of Ports* for $40 – 1-1/2 ounces each of a 40-year-old Tawny, a 1970 and a 1977 Vintage Port — or *Classic Ports* for $30 – 1-1/2 ounces each of a 20-year-old Tawny, a 1985 and a 1994 Vintage Port.

"We sell a boatload of Port wine, even through the summer," says Gambuzza. "Wines and spirits are not confined to 'a season' any more. People are more comfortable in themselves and don't feel that they have to let the outside climate dictate what they will eat and drink inside our climate-controlled dining room, bar and upstairs cigar club. Cognac and cigars have year-round appeal. I've just cracked the fifth bottle of Remy Martin XO since last January and 1999 still has three months to go."

There is a small but steady demand for grappa. Jacopo Poli Chiara Moscato and Jacopo Poli Amorasa Merlot are popular and Ashes will go through about two bottles of each in a month.

Martinis get a very strong call and the king still is the Cosmopolitan. Since Ashes opened in June 1998 the best selling specialty martinis have been *Keywest-Tini,* Stoli Ohranj, Parrot Bay Rum, Midori, Peach Schnapps with orange and cranberry juices; *Chocolate Lovers Tini,* Stoli Vanil, with Kahlua and dark crème de cacao topped with chocolate shavings; and *Little Elvis,* Absolut Mandarin, Absolut Citron, crème de cassis, sour mix and cranberry juice.

Special Dinners

Chef Gary Gross prepares special wine and cigar dinners ten times a year. Held in the upstairs Cigar Club, each attracts about 60 people. Hand-rolled cigars, fine wines and after dinner drinks are accompanied by a creative selection of foods. An unusual dinner featuring Port wines with every course was presented on October 27, 1999.

Adrian Bridge, director of Taylor Fladgate & Fonseca, was present for the event.

— The Menu —

House smoked oysters in chilled tomato consommé with basil oil
Fonseca Sirocco White Port

Pan seared foie gras on a dried fruit gastrique
Toasted brioche with apple wafers
Taylor Fladgate 20-year-old Tawny
Fonseca 7-9-9 Connecticut shade cigar

Venison Osso Bucco w/sweet potato gnocchi
and braised red cabbage
Taylor Fladgate Late Bottled Vintage 1994

Assortment of fine cheeses
Fonseca Vintage 1985 and Taylor
Fladgate Vintage 1985
Fonseca 8-9-8 Maduro cigar

The debut of
Fonseca Vintage 1997 and Taylor Fladgate Vintage 1997
Fonseca 50-50 Maduro cigar

Assortment of chocolate truffles

13 Take a Fresh Look at Your Beverage Program

"THE AMERICAN hospitality industry has always been on the cutting edge of consumer tastes," says Andrea Immer, corporate director of beverage programs for Starwood Hotels & Resorts Worldwide, Inc. "For many years American hoteliers and restaurateurs defined what was fashionable in food, wine and cocktails. Now it is the American *consumer* who is defining what is fashionable."

Immer believes that it is very important to your business that you understand that this is a sea-change that is not going to recede. Your customers want everything . . . now.

This is a great opportunity. Know who your customers are and what they want. Expand the choices you are offering them, including higher quality products at higher, but fair, prices. Train your staff in product knowledge and presentation skills.

"People eat and drink with their eyes," Immer stresses. "Serve five or six ounces of wine in a 10- or 12-ounce glass so it can be swirled and nosed before tasting. If customers ask for you to fill the glass, explain that filling a large glass halfway actually enhances the wine."

Likewise, when you serve special martinis, seek out unusual glassware to draw attention to your star drinks. Z-stem glasses are particularly eye-catching. We know what Hurricane glasses do for daiquiris and piña coladas. Immer advises that we expand our creativity across the board.

New Direction for Martinis

The creator of a wide array of flavorful martinis when she was beverage director of Windows On The World, Immer believes it is time to eliminate those specialty martinis that aren't selling and replace them with a new martini category — using high quality wine in place of vermouth.

"Very few martini drinkers care for the flavor of vermouth, hence we hear calls for 10-to-1 martinis, in-and-out martinis, just-pour-the-vodka-on-the-rocks martinis," she says. "Instead of vermouth, add Madeira, sherry, Lillet and other delicious wine-based products to premium vodkas and gins — and not just a dollop. To have the flavor come through, the ratio should be three parts vodka or gin to one part of the wine product. This is the next martini trend."

An example of this is the popularity of the *WOW Martini* at Windows On The World — Finlandia vodka and Blandy's 5-year-old Sercial Madeira.

Non-Alcohol Drinks

"We are developing an exciting array of non-alcohol drinks that will change with the seasons," Immer says. "Why miss parts of the day when guests don't care for an alcohol drink — breakfast, lunch and mid-afternoon? Also, why not cater to those who don't wish an alcohol drink for whatever reason? We will only use top quality ingredients and fresh juices so guests will perceive the value in these offerings."

Quickly becoming an "I want one of those" drinks is *Rain Forest Tea.* Brewed mint and green tea are combined with pineapple juice, orange sections and mint, shaken and served in a tall glass. Its celadon green color is an eye catcher.

"We have a tea sommelier — the first ever to my knowledge — at the New York W Hotel, and we will be expanding this concept into other of our properties," Immer adds.

Wine

Starwood Hotels owns or manages 220 hotel properties in North America. Its brand names include Sheraton, W Hotels, Four Points by Sheraton, Westin and The Luxury Collection Hotels, including the St. Regis in New York City.

"My major initiative for 2000 is the implementation of a wine training program for all servers and restaurant management staff in Starwood's North America properties," Immer confides. "We are developing 40 of our top food and beverage employees around the country into Starwood's 'Wine Posse,' trainers who will visit these properties and conduct four 45-minute sessions over the course of one month. One module will be about wine grapes and others about wine styles, wine service and wine sales."

Concurrently, she is setting up a core wine list for the properties that gives each a suggested mix of wine categories, a list of wines to choose from and suggested pricing. Individual food and beverage directors will use their discretion in deciding what, if any, additional wines make sense for their property.

"With the diversity of properties and markets that we operate in," Immer notes, "we have established four tiers of wine sophistication. Tier A properties will list 12 wines; Tier B properties will list 30 wines; Tier C properties will list 50 wines and Tier D properties will list 75 wines. No restaurant needs more than 75 wines, unless that restaurant wants to be a destination for its wine selections."

Obviously Windows On The World fits that category as do many others. Her advice to the remainder is to determine what level of wine sophistication their current customers exhibit and develop a wine list that will move them up a couple of notches.

"Train your staff so that they are knowledgeable enough to talk about wine with your guests and are confident enough that they can suggest a step-up wine that they would likely enjoy," she says. "Today's consumers are indulgence-minded, so offer them something to indulge in."

Immer, one of only nine American women to hold the title of Master Sommelier, feels that merlot is fast becoming a generic red wine, quite similar to cabernet sauvignon in body and tannin levels. "Every list should begin with one or more pinot noirs (light red), merlots (medium red) and cabernet sauvignons (full bodied)," Immer says, referring to red wines. "Steakhouses and Mediterranean restaurants would do well to list one or more red zinfandels — a wine that stands up well to their type of fare. Just be certain that staff and customers understand that this is a full-bodied, spicy red wine, not the ubiquitous white zinfandel."

Another advantage to red zinfandels is that prices are still reasonable and you can offer good value to your guests. "The next hot varietal from California will be syrah," Immer adds. "We have accepted this grape in Australian wines and when Americans try what California is producing, they will react favorably to the more balanced and refined quality of the native product. Take the lead. Seduce your customers with finer wines that tempt them to step up a notch or two."

Part Three

Today's young servers are confused about their role in selling and serving alcoholic beverages. They have been inundated with messages that say drinking is bad for you. I have to point out that alcohol is not cocaine or heroin. Social drinking has been an acceptable part of our culture since colonial times (even during the Prohibition era).
— Deven Black

They want their drinks sexy and glamorous. Instead of a martini, they might order a Tartini . . . not just a Margarita but a Grand Margarita.
— Brian Matzkow

Microbrewery restaurants or brewpubs are not guaranteed success because of the unique brews we produce. We can never rest on our laurels. Each day our challenge is to deliver more value to our guests than they expect.
— Don Sullivan

A Lounge Menu Built Around Caviar

"THERE IS a time to change. For New York's venerable "21" Club, which operated all through Prohibition and ever since, that time was at the end of 1997. By relocating support staff to another part of the restaurant, the barroom was considerably expanded and the additional space converted into a lounge. This also allowed the bar itself to be extended, around the new bend in the room.

Newly ensconced Executive Chef Erik Blauberg then worked on developing a "21" Club Lounge Menu. This did not happen overnight. Blauberg totally immerses himself in a project before he comes up with a game plan. Almost 25 years before coming to the "21" Club, he worked in the kitchens of Paul Bocuse and Roger Verge, followed by stints in the kitchens at the Imperial Hotel in Tokyo and Kicho in Osaka. Back in the United States, he worked in the kitchens of Bouley, La Côte Basque, Windows On the World, Tavern on the Green and more. So you can understand why, before making caviar a focal point for the new lounge menu, he decided to visit a family friend in Russia who was in the caviar business. "I went out on the fishing boats, fished myself and worked at every step in the processing of roe into caviar," recalls Blauberg today. "And when I tasted the caviar produced, as well as other local caviar, I was not happy with what I tasted."

Blauberg had learned that the key to excellence in caviar was in the salt and water used in the final processing. After extensive research he determined that the best salt in the world was sea salt from Fleur De Sel and that Switzerland had the purest water. He then arranged for the roe, sea salt and water to be shipped to a plant in Romania that then used these elements to produce his private cache of caviar.

Only then was he ready to produce the "21" Club Lounge Menu, leading off with "21" Beluga Caviar Service — $65, along with Chilled Teton Glacier Vodka, Moet & Chandon Brut N.V., Veuve Clicquot Brut N.V. There is a Daily Market Selection of Atlantic and Pacific oysters, antipasto salad with soppressata and aged provolone, crispy shrimp with ginger-citrus sauce, lobster quesadilla with avocado, lime and cilantro, and mini "21" burgers with potato straws. International cheese platter and mixed berry tartlettes with vanilla cream and berry coulis round out the 1999 selections.

From six kilos of caviar a month, sales quickly jumped to over 28 kilos, about 500 servings. Seventy percent of the time it's accompanied with vodka, 30 percent of the time with Champagne. Ninety percent of caviar sales are in the dining room or at private parties, ten percent in the lounge.

"We also offer three varieties of pita pizzas at the bar and lounge," adds Blauberg. "We top flat pitas with an unusual variety of toppings, that also taste good. Tonight we have a vegetarian combination, a carpacio of tuna with arugula greens and a filet mignon presentation. Another time we'll top a pita with our "21" Club burger mix."

From 5 p.m. to 7 p.m., the bar is packed three or more deep. As the bar crowd thins out, the lounge tables are filling up. "Everybody ends up in the lounge," says Blauberg, "and if they are hungry, they expect the food to live up to '21' Club standards. My job is to see that it does."

Wine Cellar Dinners

In the center of the wine cellar is a dinner table that can seat up to 20 people. It is occupied six nights a week, and is booked for lunch three to four days a week, for private functions. A Wine Dinner Series, open to the public, is always quickly sold out. The 1998 events opened with a Joseph Phelps Wine dinner under the direction of Executive Chef Erik Blauberg and Wine Director Christopher Shipley.

Hors d'oeuvres were accompanied by Voignier Vin du Mistral 1996. Pan-seared lobster with winter vegetables and tomato risotto was paired with Chardonnay Ovation 1995. Oak-fried squab with warm black lentil salad and crisp shallots was paired with Le Mistral 1995. Spit-roasted lamb chops with Yuca purée and lamb jus was matched with Insignia 1994. Port-braised oxtail with chive-mashed potatoes and fried leeks was paired with Cabernet Sauvignon Backus 1991 and Eisele 1991. Lemon pudding with flambé of mixed berries was paired with Johannisberg Riesling Special Select Late Harvest 1989.

The cost was $400 per person, all inclusive.

15 It's All About Image

"IN THE bursting-with-energy, 'hot' bars in Manhattan it's all about image," smiles Brian Matzkow, food and beverage director for the SoHo Grand Hotel.

"Dom Perignon, Krug Grande Cuvée and Louis Roederer Cristal are all excellent Champagnes, all selling around the $200 price point. But it's Cristal, the most expensive at $225, that we see prominently positioned on tables in the Grand Bar — about 60 times a month. The bottle is immediately recognizable and makes a statement about the people at that table."

Opening in 1996, the Soho Grand Hotel was the first hotel built in SoHo in over a hundred years. It quickly became the center of attraction for the area's burgeoning creative industries — computers, the Internet, fashion, photography and the arts. For many in these industries the hotel makes a statement about who they are and what they are.

"The Grand Bar is a meeting place for people looking to have a fun evening," says Matzkow. "They want their drinks sexy and glamorous. Instead of a martini they might order a *Tartini* — Stoli Razberi, Chambord and cranberry juice. Not just a Margarita but a *Grand Margarita* — Sauza Conmemorativo tequila, Cointreau, fresh lime and orange juice." These cocktails are served in seven-ounce martini glasses, filled to the brim. Approximately 15 high-end wines are offered by the glass. Servers partially fill a large wineglass, then pour more wine into a side decanter, for seven ounces in total. Guests can swirl the wine, make a show of nosing it and share tastes with others at their table. Very cosmopolitan!

Cognac bottles are placed on the table, along with a giant snifter. The server pours up to the two-ounce line of a measured beaker, pours this into the snifter and then pours another ounce into the beaker. "Everything is presentation and perception," adds Matzkow. "Our servers are very accommodating, very knowledgeable and give great service with a smile . . . and a slight attitude."

Not every Champagne drinker orders Cristal. Veuve Clicquot, priced at $14 for a glass and $36 for a half-bottle, gets the big play. Under development are new drinks that will be designed to evoke a ripple of, "Hey, what's that?" and sharing drinks for couples. "Everything is marketing. The price of the wine dictates the glassware presented with it," says Matzkow.

Drinking First, Eating After

Recognizing a trend towards exotic foods served in smaller, tasty portions, the Canal House restaurant across from the bar is now more lounge-like and less formal, offering caviar and other high-end foods in a fashion that encourages sharing. A party of six will sometimes order eight different items to share, while they are drinking, chatting and laughing. Trendy, upscale "tray" tables bring the dining table to the salon, which is positioned between the restaurant and the bar.

"Our goal is to make the guest happy," Matzkow concludes. "Shortly, we'll be bringing that philosophy to the new Tribeca Grand Hotel opening in March 2000."

16 Tequila is More Than Margaritas

IN 1995, Nelson Portela and his management team of GM Eddie McGhie and manager Pedro Hernandez realized they were not going to increase bar revenues by selling more drinks to each customer. "My restaurant, The Alamo, was very respected for its authentic Mexican food and Margaritas," he recalls, "and traditionally we sold a lot of Margaritas. But the trend towards more moderate drinking was affecting our bottom line."

Rather than trying to increase profits by raising prices, they determined to make the New York City restaurant as famous for the high quality tequilas it offered as it was for the exceptional quality of its cuisine.

Entering the year 2000, The Alamo offered over 120 tequilas, and sipping tequilas accounted for 20 percent of tequila sales. That percentage edges up every month. Prices for a one-and-a-half ounce drink range from $5 to $140 for José Cuervo Collecion, a limited edition of only 347 bottles, each in a magnificent leather box.

Capitalizing on Unique Packaging

"Fine Mexican craftsmanship is reflected in the packaging of many tequila brands and it makes no sense to position them on the back bar for decoration only," stresses Portela. "Bartenders and servers present them to our guests and explain what makes these tequilas special and worth what we are charging for them. Tequila Añejo Casta, Weber Azul, 100 percent blue agave, is packaged in a wide-mouthed bottle with a cork stopper. Our waiters bring this to the table, remove the cork and suggest that each person inhale the aroma while they then extol its virtues."

Don Julio añejo, 100 percent blue agave, is presented on a swivel stand. When a guest requests a serving at the bar or at a table, the bottled is tilted and poured from the stand in front of the guest. This provokes oohs and aahs from others in the room, or at the bar, and a chorus of: "I want that."

Other unique packages that are personally presented to guests include: El Mayor Reserve, packed in a wooden box with a rope handle, $8 per drink, and Porfidio Barrique, packaged in a tall, slim bottle with a glass cactus inside, $40 per drink.

"In a slow month we will empty twelve Patrón bottles," says Portela. "After thorough cleaning, these rustic, hand-blown bottles are filled with balsamic vinegar and virgin olive oil with herbs and placed on dining room tables. Almost everybody asks for the next empty bottle and we accommodate them as best we can."

Requests also pour in for other unique bottles, which become available less often. The most frequent customers have an edge here, but Portela is considering other ways to distribute the high-demand bottles that will reward the customers who order the specific brand frequently.

What Tequila to Choose?

Looking at The Alamo's tequila selections from a bar stool can be rather daunting. Where do you start? Fortunately, knowledgeable bartenders come to the rescue by presenting the complete tequila list and opening a dialogue about which tequilas might suit a particular customer's taste.

Frequently, the bartender will suggest a flight of three tequilas, one-half ounce each, either a starter set of Porfidio single-barrel añejo, Gran Centenario reposado and Lapiz reposado for $15 or a flight of José Cuervo Reserva de la Familia añejo, Herradurra Selecion Suprema and Don Eduardo añejo for $35. Another option is a customized three-tequila selection to fit the customer's preferences.

A Solution to a Problem

At one time, tequila shots were served in specialty pony glasses that were frequently taken for souvenirs. Some of you are no doubt familiar with this phenomenon. Portela came up with a solution — trim the bottom of a lime so it will stand upright on the bar. Cut the top quarter off the lime, extracting the juice for Margaritas and leaving some pulp in the bottom. Arrange the limes on a serving tray, fill with chilled tequila or tequila concoctions, put the tray on the bar and serve tequila shots. Anybody wishing to keep the spent lime for a souvenir may do so.

Flavor, Flavor, Flavor

With flavored tequilas, such as tequila rose, gaining in popularity, The Alamo has been increasing its supply of barrels for on-premise aging of flavored white tequilas.

"Our oak barrels range in size from one to eight liters. Most are Mexican barrels previously used to age tequila and our latest came from Spain where it was used for aging sherry" Portela says. "We'll add cinnamon, kiwi, oranges, herbs or herbs and nuts to a non-aged Herradurra, Sauza or Patrón and age them for two to eight months, frequently tasting to determine when each flavor reaches its peak."

A white El Tesoro is aged, with no added flavoring, for four to six months in an eight-liter barrel that sits on the back bar. Once tapped, this *Alamo Tequila* barrel will be emptied in two to three months and customers will wait impatiently for the next batch to be ready.

It's Show Time

Hanging above the bar is a large glass pitcher with a long pouring spout. It's not just a decoration. Every night, at 7 p.m., the pitcher is filled with tequila, pineapple juice, orange juice and a splash of 7-Up. Willing customers tilt their heads back, open their mouths and trust to the aim of the bartender, now standing on the bar and poised to pour an *Alamo Splash* down their throats until they raise their arms to signal that it's enough. A cloth napkin protects clothing from an errant delivery and most nights 10 to 15 people can participate. Portela does remember one or two times when the contents of the pitcher did not get past the first willing participant. Generally 40 or 50 people will participate in an evening's Splash party.

The Alamo Splash is also a dining room ritual on Thursday and Friday evenings and when there is a party group.

The five or six times a year that the kitchen is running late with lunch orders, it's the Alamo Splash to the rescue. "We bring that pitcher into the room and go from table to table while Mexican music is playing loudly and everybody's having so much fun they don't care when they get their food," laughs Portela.

This practice of drinking from a "porron" originated in the poor regions in the south of Spain and allowed people to gather in a group and drink without the need of costly glassware. It was, and is, quite sanitary since nobody's lips touch the pitcher's spout.

Another crowd-pleaser is *The Alamo Fiesta Bowl,* first presented in the winter of 1998/99. Picture a clay bowl, warmed, with six cups hanging along its rim. Pour in a half bottle of white tequila, add sugar, ten coffee beans and fruit — oranges, kiwi, strawberries, mango or whatever. Well away from customers, light the mixture and stir while flaming. The fire burns off much of the alcohol, leaving a rich, concentrated, great tasting liqueur. When made at the bar, it's sold as individual drinks (generally producing five or six servings). At tables, it is prepared for groups of four or more.

Four times a year a prix fixe four-course tequila dinner is offered, each course paired with a tequila that best complements it. A host gives a short talk about tequila and the bottles being tasted, and knowledgeable servers answer any questions guests may have. At $60 these dinners are quickly sold out.

Not Just Tequila

"The Alamo is the largest restaurant account in New York for Torres wines from Spain," says Portela proudly. "These wines complement Mexican food exquisitely. We'll sell four cases a month of Sangre de Toro (Blood of Bull) red wine and five cases a month of Vina Sol white wine."

Waiters always ask if diners would like wine with their meal. Most guests have no idea what wine would be appropriate and listen attentively to what their server has to say about how a particular wine would enhance an appetizer or entrée.

When guests order a second bottle of the same wine, they are given fresh glasses. "Even with the same wine, flavors can vary subtly," he says. "We also provide a fresh glass whenever a guest orders another drink."

A new feature in the dining room is a specially designed cart for tableside cooking with tequila.

How Do Servers Get So Smart?

"It's amazing how much impact solid training has on retaining good waiters and bartenders," says Portela. "Since I opened The Alamo in 1986, in addition to a short meeting daily on food and drink specials, we have had a weekly, 30-minute training meeting. For 20 minutes we study everything about tequila, from planting the agave to harvesting, distillation, aging and packaging, as part of a four-month course. For the next ten minutes we discuss three tequilas specifically and some of our food specialties — what ingredients are in the dishes and how each is prepared.

"Once a month, we have a two-hour meeting that features industry representatives talking about their products in depth, as well as input from the chef on what is happening in the kitchen. A 30-minute staff brainstorming session explores what could be done to expand sales."

Most recently, bartender Antonio Lara took a piece from an antique Mexican dresser and combined strips of pewter with turquoise and gold paint to spell out "TEQUILA" on it. Affixing a rustic, multi-colored cowboy rope, he hung the handcrafted sign on the back bar above the section for premium tequilas.

This enthusiasm sparks an energy that customers pick up and feed back to the staff and everybody has a good time.

"Our four bartenders and eight waiters are proud of what they do," says Portela. "Their knowledge of the foods and beverages that we serve is so extensive that they welcome questions from our guests, who are then pleasantly surprised to get intelligent answers instead of the ubiquitous: 'I'll ask the chef or manager.' Three of our staff have been with us for 12 years, the rest, except one, have been here for more than four years. Our newest staff member has been here for over a year."

Besides the training that allows each staff member to be proud of his or her job knowledge, an equally important factor in keeping turnover so low is that everybody is treated with respect. Portela lets his staff know that he appreciates their efforts. Staff opinions are solicited and acted upon. Earnings are good, and perks are given for the top tequila seller each month.

New York's "Authentic" British Pub

"TO MY knowledge, the North Star Pub is the only authentic British pub on this side of the Atlantic," says GM Deven Black. "We only serve British beers on tap, 50 kegs a week of the eight varieties, another 14 brands of bottled beer and over 75 single malt Scotches."

With just 1,250 square feet of space and no basement, it's a wonder that there is room for 30 table seats and another 30 seats at the bar.

Up to 72 back-up beer kegs are stored in cooler space sublet at a working fish stall in the nearby Fulton Fish Market and back-up cases of wines, liquors and bottled British beers are in storage space in a building across the street.

"From our opening day in 1983, we had to concentrate on building high traffic at all times of the day, not just traditional meal hours," stresses Black.

South Street Seaport, one of Manhattan's prime tourist attractions in the summer months, provides abundant walk-by prospects for half the year. Black's challenge was to entice them to stop in, then to develop a plan that would not only bring them back in the cooler months, but also draw a following from outside the pub's immediate area.

Noting the rising popularity of single malt Scotch whisky, he decided to make this a specialty. Not having the space for formal tastings, he created a self-guided Single Malt Scotch Tasting Menu designed to "help you discover the intricate and pleasurable world of single malt Scotch. We suggest that you 'nose' these whiskies before tasting them. To nose whisky: exhale, place the glass under your nose, then inhale through your mouth. You will get the full aroma of the whisky, without any harshness."

Tasting #1: A tour of Scotland. $11.00

Each of the three major distilling areas of Scotland produces a particular style of whisky. The Lowland malts are lighter while Highland malts are more elegant and well rounded. Islay (pronounced: eye-luh) malts tend to be briny and very peaty.

Lowland: Glenkinchie 10 year old.
Highland: Royal Lochnagan 12 year old.
Islay: Bunnahahbain 12 year old.

Tasting #2: Laphroaig, backwards. $25.00

"Most of the time we would taste a single distillery's malts from the youngest to the oldest," notes Black, "but not with tangy Laphroaig. Taste these in the order we suggest and you'll understand why we save the young one for last."

Laphroaig 30, 15 and 10 year old.

Tasting #3: Defenders of the Malt. $11.00

Hiram Walker, which imports these three whiskies and designed the "Defenders of the Malt" theme as a marketing ploy, says tasting them side by side shows how both geographic location and the craftsmanship of the distiller turns what starts out as simple malted barley into surprisingly distinct end products.

Scapa 12 year old.
Glendronach 15 year old.
Laphroaig 10 year old.

Tasting #4: The Macallans. $15.00

Macallan recently introduced Gran Reserva, an 18 year old, aged in first-fill oloroso sherry butts. Compare it with whiskies more typical of the Macallan house style.

Macallan 12 year old.
Macallan 18 year old.
Macallan 18 year old Gran Reserva.

Tasting #4A: Add an even older Macallan. $30.00

The above three plus Macallan 25 year old.

Page two of the menu lists available single malt Scotches classified as: Light to Medium Bodied Malts, Medium Bodied Malts, Medium to Full Bodied Malts, Full Bodied Malts. Prices per serving range from $6.00 to $30.00 for a 1.75-ounce drink. Tastings are a half-shot of each brand.

While this emphasis on single malt Scotches quickly drew a loyal clientele that was steadily increased by strong word-of-mouth, Black is not one to put all of his drinks in one basket.

"As proprietors of a British pub we decided to celebrate the products and traditions of Britain in a typically British way — tongue-in-cheek humor and a poke in the eye of pomposity," he says. The pub's newsletter of December 1993 proclaimed:

> "Christmas is coming, and that means Boxing Day is near. We'll be holding our tenth annual Boxing Day party on Saturday, December 26, starting at 11:30 a.m. Make no mistake about it. We're celebrating Boxing Day on the traditional day after Christmas.
>
> "We're not giving in to the modernist forces who have persuaded the homeland to 'observe' Boxing Day on Monday the 28th. We 'observe' daylight savings time. We celebrate Boxing Day right where it has been celebrated for centuries, the day after Christmas.
>
> "We start the day off with our second annual St. Stephen's Day Mass celebrated, using the North Star bar as the altar, by our own Father Mac and the members of the Holy Name Parish of North Bergen, New Jersey. All are welcome to this service of Thanksgiving starting at 10:30 a.m.
>
> "At 11:30 we start the world's largest and most generous Boxing Day party. *(NOTE: typical British understatement is typically suspended for the holidays)*. Everyone gets a free Christmas cracker containing a joke, a toy and a silly hat we make you wear. Once again we'll have free Bangers and Mash, more than 500 pounds of it, available while the supply lasts. Sing-alongs and Yard of Ale contests will add to the festivities, all sponsored by Grolsch Importers of Atlanta, the wonderful people who bring us the delicious prize-winning ales: Fuller's London Pride and Fuller's E.S.B."

The 1998 newsletter saluted that year's sponsor: Scottish and Newcastle Importers and concluded with:

> "We must warn you, however, that Boxing Day has become extremely popular and the pub gets very loud and crowded. If you enjoy a boisterous good time, this is the place to be on December 26th. But if you like a quiet drink and time to think, you'd better come some other time."

The newsletter's monthly calendar calls attention to bits of British trivia that Americans would otherwise be deprived of, at great personal loss. Did you know that Britain's first satellite, the oddly named Ariel III, was launched in California, where the weather is better, on May 5, 1967? Hellston Cornwall holds an annual Furry Dance in May? Henry VIII married Jane Seymour, wife III of VI, a mere XI days after wife II, Anne Boleyn was executed, on May XXX, MDXXXVI?

Festive events are concocted around some of these dates. For example, the North Star Pub celebrated the fiftieth anniversary of England's declaration of war on Germany by converting the premises into a "1939 pub/recruiting station." Special menus featured powdered egg omelets and meatless shepherd's pie. Blackout rules were in effect and Vera Lynn and Winston Churchill were on the radio.

On the last night of this three-night gala, women were invited to compete to see who could paint the straightest stocking seams on their legs with an eyebrow pencil.

"We are alert to every possible British tie-in to current events," adds Black. "During the recent World Cup soccer matches we ran a promotion with Boddington's Pub Ale and gave away, in a drawing, a replica of the 1966 British World Cup Jersey every day that Britain was competing."

They also gave prizes to customers for the most accurate guesses of the total number of goals in the tournament, the total number of red cards, the goal totals for the British team and so forth.

Non-British promotions also surface occasionally. As a favor to a supplier, Black ordered one bottle of Hot Sex, a new prepared cocktail made from imported Canton ginger liqueur, vodka, cream, chocolate, ginseng and what the label calls "other natural flavors." It didn't sell.

On page one of the March/April 1998 newsletter Black headlined a story — "Try Hot Sex at a Special Price." After romancing readers with a fantasy tale, the feature ended with: "To break down your inhibitions, for a limited time — as long as the bottle lasts — we'll be selling Hot Sex for $1.00 a shot. If it meets with approval, we'll get more. If not, it is the last hot sex you'll ever get here."

It sold . . . so well that he reordered and reordered for about a five-month run. It didn't become a runaway best seller but it did keep conversation going at the bar in a light vein. And customers did enjoy the drink, at a more profitable pricing of $2.00 per shot on Wednesdays and Thursdays during May and June, regular prices on other days.

A New North Star Pub?

At this writing, John Belle, owner of the North Star Pub, is considering expanding into a vacant next-door space. This would increase table seating to 110 and allow for the expansion of its spirits and beer offerings. Belle, the architect responsible for the recent magnificent renewal of Grand Central Terminal, is determined to maintain the overall look and appeal of the smaller pub if this expansion takes place. The menu would be broadened to embrace the foods of former British colonies. "Assuming England listened more closely to its colonies and learned from them as much as it tried to instruct them, this is the food you might be eating in London today," Black says rather sardonically.

Since the central part of that trade was rum, there will be an increased emphasis on fine sipping rums as well as the exotic beers from India, Jamaica, Africa and Singapore.

"There would be room for sit-down tastings, not only of single malt Scotches but also of sipping rums, super premium vodkas and other beverage categories that interest our guests," he adds.

"After adjusting our sea legs, we would enter a second stage, expanding into larger selections of sherries and Ports, perhaps an authentic replication of an outstanding beer from colonial America. I am sure the next 15 years will be as exciting — and surprising — as the first 15."

The Importance of Staff Education

"Today's young servers are confused about their role in selling and serving alcoholic beverages. They have been inundated with messages that say drinking is bad for you," Black asserts. "I have to point out that alcohol is not cocaine or heroin. Social drinking has been an acceptable part of our culture since colonial times (even during the Prohibition era).

"Consumed in moderation, alcohol has been proven to be a healthful part of a diet for most people. It can be abused and some people have to stay away from it for health reasons. Staff should be alert to these situations and we train them on how to serve these guests appropriately."

Realizing that young servers can not be expected to be personally knowledgeable about every spirit offered at the pub, Black has prepared primers about single malt Scotches and other spirits to provide this information to his staff in an easily digestible form. He also holds staff tastings accompanied by learned and interesting spokespeople.

Staff members who don't want to ingest alcohol are asked to "taste by smell." You can learn about a spirit by pouring a small amount into a snifter, swirling it and then holding the glass to your nose.

Seventeen years away from the stick, Black vividly remembers the management style of Dan Hickey, GM of an Upper West Side restaurant/bar called Shelter. Black was the bartender when Hickey was sitting at the bar with the two owners. As the bar got exceedingly busy, he heard one of the owners tell Hickey to get him some help. "No, watch," said Hickey. Hearing that vote of confidence Black pulled out all the stops, handling the crowd with aplomb.

"Trust," he says now. "Trust your people to perform and they won't let you down. Your staff will make mistakes. Help them learn from them. Don't scream; don't apply pressure; don't create problems."

I believe it's appropriate to end this chapter with a page that appears in most issues of North Star Pub Notes.

— Potables —

A publican stood at the Golden Gate,
His head was bent and low.
He meekly asked the man of Fate
which way he had to go.
"What have you done?" St. Peter said
"To seek admission here?"
I kept a public house below
for many and many a year.
St. Peter opened wide the gate
and gently pressed the bell.
"Come inside and choose your harp
you've had your share of hell.

— Anonymous

18 The Microbrewery Challenge

"HAVING HELPED design and install kitchens in three new brewpubs in Manhattan and Westchester, I became hooked on the idea of opening a restaurant that also made and served the best, cleanest and highest quality beers that could be made," says Don Sullivan.

Sullivan had been a chef at restaurants on Long Island and in New York since 1984. His brother, Kevin, was a beverage manager for the Doral Hotel in Manhattan, after a two-year stint at the Doral in Telluride, Colorado. Another brother, Jim, is a businessman in Manhattan who had worked as a bartender and waiter to help pay college expenses.

"When the opportunity arose in 1996 to take over the Southampton, Long Island, property that had housed the legendary Herb McCarthy's Bowden Square Restaurant, we decided this was the time and place to open our microbrewery restaurant," Sullivan continued. "Our goal was to establish a casual dining, neighborhood restaurant where families would be comfortable, perceiving they were receiving good value for their money. And, not so incidentally, drinking the finest international style brews that could be crafted."

The brothers knew it would be tough. Brewpubs and microbrewery restaurants have had a high failure rate in the New York area, especially on Long Island, where people drive to restaurants and are especially conscious of DWI laws.

After Herb McCarthy retired, there had been a succession of restaurant concepts tried at the location — all failures. For the previous seven years the restaurants had closed in October and reopened in May, effectively making a statement that their concern was for the summer visitors, not the locals.

This would change.

A Five-Year Plan

While extensive alterations were done to accommodate a state-of-the-art microbrewery, Don and Kevin relocated to Southampton and worked hard at becoming active members of the year-round community.

Before opening The Southampton Publick House, Don requested a meeting with the Village Board where he introduced himself as a new member of the business community, offering the facilities of the restaurant for use by government and community groups as needed.

Ten days prior to opening, community groups were taking Sullivan up on his offer of hospitality. A week before the late-June opening, a two-hour cocktail party was held for local businessmen and government employees. Three days later, a similar bash was held for all of the contractors, suppliers and workmen involved in the renovation work.

"This gave local people the opportunity of tasting our food and some of our beers in a non-critical way," Don says. "We also had a chance to iron out the kinks in service and mechanical areas that always surface on opening a new restaurant.

"We began with a five-year plan that included buying the brewery outright and paying for all renovations in the first three months," adds Don. "Opening in mid-season, we had an immediate cash flow that helped meet the heavy, unexpected expenses that came out of left field in the fall — a disaster with the heating system being particularly costly.

"Now we began reaping benefits from our involvement with the community. Year round we book four to five catering events a week in the restaurant, for 30 or more people for each event. This has allowed us to maintain a core staff of about 25 people through the year, adding another 15 staff members for the summer season, generally teachers and college students with summers free."

The Sullivans took the approach that they were merging a different type of entertainment into a neighborhood restaurant. Dining room guests could view the glassed-enclosed Brew House where the beer is made, in a museum-style presentation. Tap Room guests view the fermentation tanks on display behind the bar. Serving tanks are out of sight below the bar. The room was designed to be a place to meet friends before or after dinner in an atmosphere similar to that of a hotel bar. Casual foods are available until 10 p.m., 11 p.m. on weekends, every day except Christmas.

"While we want to be known as a fine neighborhood restaurant, we take great pride in our microbrewery," Don points out. "Our brewing tanks and equipment were built and installed by Diversified Metal Engineers, a Canadian firm well respected for their expertise. Consulting Brewmaster Jack Streich oversaw the design and installation of the system to produce premium international style beers in the style of Bass Ale, Heineken, Pilsner Urquel, etcetera."

Forty-five days before opening, nationally acclaimed brewmaster Phil Markowski was hired to create and produce the beers to be served. He also writes about beer and serves as a judge at craft beer competitions.

Year-round Brews in 1999

Southampton Golden Lager — brewed in the Munich style, lagered for 6 weeks.

Montauk Light — a light but full-flavored lager, about 110 calories per glass.

East End India Pale Ale — authentic English-style amber ale with a unique character that comes from a secret blend of four hop varieties and the use of imported English malts.

Publick House Porter — Markowski's version of original "London-style" porter, made with 5 different malts and two varieties of hops.

Southampton Secret Ale — a special secret Alt beer, a north German ale with a malty flavor and a refreshing hop bitterness, brewed with five varieties of German malt and imported German hops.

Seasonal Brews in 1999

Throughout the year, two seasonal beers are on tap at all times.

Winter: Imperial Stout, very potent Russian-style French Country Christmas Ale, a high potent sipping beer

Spring: Sullivan's Irish Ale, an amber, lighter style ale; *McSully's Dry Stout,* St. Patrick's Day only, considerably lighter than the Imperial Stout.

Summer: Black Raspberry Wheat Beer, Belgian-style wheat beer and *Old New York-style Pilsner*, similar to the crisp, clean, light lager produced by Schaefer Brewing.

Vintage Beer Cellar

The Beer Cellar is not a separate room in the restaurant, but rather a state of mind. An ever-changing variety of exotic brews, generally higher in alcohol content, are vintage dated and hand bottled primarily in "Champagne" bottles and served in specialty glassware. Some offerings have been:

Peconic County Reserve Ale, brewed with Chardonnay grapes from Sag Pond Vineyards 1996 vintage.

Peconic County Reserve Ale, same as above, 1998 vintage.

Southampton Saison Cuvée Speciale, a Belgian-style farmhouse ale flavored with spices and four varieties of edible flowers.

Southampton "Double" Ice Bock, an extremely strong, yet smooth and malty "Ice Bock" fortified by freezing the brew at zero degrees Fahrenheit, estimated to have 18 percent alcohol by volume.

Planned introductions include *Imperial Baltic Porter, French "Bière de Garde," Belgian Grand Cru Strong, Belgian Double White Ale.*

Outside Beer Sales

A substantial amount of keg beer, mostly *Southampton Secret Ale,* is sold through beer wholesalers to high-end restaurants, hotels and clubs on Long Island and in New York City. Beer bars, some with 30 or 40 taps, are especially good customers for seasonal beers.

A Happening Place

During the summer season, a DJ keeps the Tap Room humming on weekend nights after 10 p.m. Acoustic music, solos and duos, bring locals in on weekend nights during the off-season. A Valentine's Day Lingerie Show has become a major fundraiser for the South Fork Breast Health Coalition. About 300 people are in and out as local people, including some celebrities, model the latest fashions for the benefit of breast cancer research and education.

"Halloween, Octoberfest, Thanksgiving, Brunch with Santa are just some of the promotions that give people another reason to visit us," says Kevin Sullivan. "The wineries often recommend us to their visitors because they know we will not disappoint them. We do have a selective wine list and a half dozen of the selections are Long Island wines."

"Microbrewery restaurants or brewpubs are not guaranteed success because of the unique brews we produce," chimes in Don. "We can never rest on our laurels. Each day our challenge is to deliver more value to our guests than they expect."

Part Four

Promotions bring people in and hospitality brings them back.
— Monte Silva

The key for us is staff training. We have to be the tequila experts even if some staff members have never tasted sipping tequila before joining us. Just as important as location, location, location is training, training, training.
— Phil Barragato

We set an authentic tone, with our vast array of photos of the Irish people and places and our antiques collection, but it's the people who have adopted The Irish Bank as their pub that have given us our personality.
— Rory Connolly

Our kitchen is open until midnight, sometimes later, and our signature food special, Lobster Shepherd's Pie, is so popular that people fear we may eat the lobsters into extinction.
— Chris Martin

Twice a month, on Fridays between shifts, managers and bartenders meet for 30 to 45 minutes to taste the new tequilas we have added and discuss them . . . Our huge amount of sipping tequilas is due to customer requests and expectations.
— Walter Carrillo

19 Hospitality Plus

"IT'S IMPORTANT to have the right person behind the bar," emphasizes Monte Silva, general manager of Wolfgang Puck Cafe in El Segundo, Califonia. "The persona we project is that Wolfgang Puck Cafe is a fun and exciting place to be. Our bartenders have to deliver on that."

When he was GM of the unit in Santa Monica, California, Silva introduced Martini Mondays at the bar, and quickly had to expand the program to include dining room customers intrigued by the jazzy looking drinks: a *Godiva Ketel One Martini* topped with shaved chocolate chips, a *Martini Sunrise* with Absolut, orange juice and a dash of grenadine, a *Blue Skyy Martini* with Skyy vodka, pineapple juice and blue curaçao, a *Radioactive Martini* with vodka and Midori.

All martinis served at the bar were complemented with a side dish of olives stuffed with blue cheese, for snacking or dunking.

Guest Bartender Night was held once a month from 8 p.m. to 11 p.m. "We'd select somebody with an outgoing personality and a lot of friends who enjoyed drinking," Silva says. "Our head bartender was at his side, helping when needed. We'd generally see 25 to 30 new faces and increase our night's bar business by about $700."

At meal times the management team visits all tables to chat with guests and assess their feelings. Are they having a good time? Are they getting good service? Everybody gets a warm "thanks for coming" when leaving. "Promotions bring people in," Silva preaches, "and hospitality brings them back."

Special Dinners

Promotions aren't confined to the bar with an occasional overflow to the dining room. Once a month a special dinner is presented at the Santa Monica location for up to 30 guests at $50 to $60 a person, including tax and tip. At El Segundo, up to 100 guests can be handled. Tables are set for 10 to 15, promoting mingling among the attendees and sometimes offering networking opportunities along with the fun.

A Martini Dinner paired a *Bombay Sapphire Martini* with a spinach Gorgonzola salad, a *Stoli Gold Martini* with the guest's choice of rosemary chicken, salmon or rib eye steak as an entrée and a *Chocolate Ketel One Martini* paired with crème brûlée for dessert.

A Single Malt Scotch Dinner offered a choice of Glenfiddich, Macallan 12 or Macallan 18 year old with butternut squash soup and chocolate soufflé for dessert. Entrées were accompanied with appropriate wines or beers.

The Tequila Dinner, which had the best turnout, paired a Sauza Conmemorativo Tequila with tortilla soup, a *Hornitos Margarita* with a combo plate of chiles rellenos, duck tamale, black beans and rice, followed by Très Generaciones served in a snifter and accompanied by a coconut flan.

"The highlight of our Rum Dinner was Macadamia Nut Liqueur, brought to my attention by Chuck Giometti, representing Hawaiian Distillers," says Silva. "For dessert we served pineapple cake with ice cream and a serving of the liqueur. Coffee was also laced with Macadamia Nut Liqueur, followed by some fine aged rums from Trinidad — Barrows Grand Reserve and Barrows Hors d'Age. Since these are 'cigar-blended rums,' cigars were available for all who wished them.

"At this time, Wolfgang Puck has nine fine dining restaurants, 16 cafes and six Expresses carrying his name, plus three Obachine Asian fine dining restaurants," he adds. "While each operation has its own personality, the Puck name tells our guests that they will receive fine food and service. The unique designs created by Barbara Lazaroff tell our guests that they are going to have fun."

At each location, it's the job of the general manager and executive chef to deliver on these promises.

20 Where Margaritas Drive the Bar Business

SIXTY-TWO different Margaritas with 62 different tequilas — that's what you can choose from when you enter Cozymel's Coastal Mexican Grill in El Segundo, California. On the back bar you'll also see ten Taylor Slurpee machines filled with a mix tailored to quickly produce a variety of flavored, frozen Margaritas.

The El Segundo location is one of 20 units in a chain that serves authentic Mexican cuisine at modest prices. The drink list on the menu offers an array of selections identical to those offered in every other Cozymel.

Margarita-ville

Top-shelf Margaritas include:

Perfect Porfidio – hand shaken and served in the traditional manner, or with prickly pear juice in a Mexican carafe for one.

Primo Rita – frozen or on the rocks with Sauza Conmemorativo, Cointreau and real juice sweet-and-sour.

José's Gold – the same drink as above, substituting José Cuervo Gold.

Meltdown Margaritas offer:

Mel's Meltdown – a traditional Margarita topped with a choice of Cointreau, Chambord, Grand Marnier or Midori.

Raz Rita – raspberry-infused tequila melted down into a traditional Margarita.

Sangria Swirl – a traditional Margarita swirled with fresh-fruit-infused sangria wine.

Traditional Margaritas include flavor variations of peach, strawberry, mango and blue curaçao.

Specialties of the House include a piña colada made with Bacardi Black and *Cozy On The Beach,* which takes the piña colada, swirls strawberries into it and tops it off with a little peach Margarita. A *Triple Bypass* is Cozymel's version of a cherry daiquiri. A non-alcohol version of this drink is also available.

Accent on Tequila

A small line on the drink list suggests that guests "ask for our other feature tequilas."

"This is when our bartenders really shine," says Walter Carrillo, manager of the El Segundo Cozymel's. "Twice a month, on Fridays between shifts, managers and bartenders meet for 30 to 45 minutes to taste the new tequilas we have added and discuss them.

"What type of a tequila is this? For a Margarita? As a shot? A martini mixer, perhaps? A shooter when mixed with liqueurs? If we don't get a unanimous consensus on a brand, we do not reorder that brand. We also determine which tequilas we will discontinue to make room for new tequilas that we decide to add permanently."

Half of the 62 tequilas carried are sipping tequilas. Some examples, along with bartenders' comments:

Arette — "So smooth it would get lost in a Margarita."
El Tesoro — ". . . just add a squeeze of lime, no salt."
Cazadores — "Extremely good in a Kamikaze, straight up."
Herradurra Añejo — ". . . with a splash of amaretto."
Cuervo Reserva La Familia — ". . . for a tequila sunrise.
It has almost all of the character of a good bourbon aged in old bourbon barrels."

Almendrado — "This almond-flavored tequila is excellent when served straight, ice cold, as a dessert tequila."

"Our huge amount of sipping tequilas is due to customer requests and expectations," says Carrillo. "We are close enough to the Mexican border that many people ask about brands they have tasted and enjoyed when in Mexico, and we do our best to accommodate them."

A non-tequila tip from Carrillo: Before making a mai tai, put in a few drops of a good Scotch.

On the Other Coast

Across the continent, Long Islanders flocking to Cozymel's in Westbury, New York, are also asking for sipping tequilas.

"Our guests don't have the same degree of tequila sophistication as do Californians," says manager Phil Barragato, "but there has been a marked increase in the demand for fine tequilas since I came to this location in 1997."

Competitions Keep Enthusiasm High

Margaritas are still the engine driving bar sales, however. Barragato keeps staff enthusiasm high by having month-long promotions of a competitive nature. One month the goal was to see how much Porfidio tequila could be sold in Margaritas and sipping portions. The answer was a resounding 2,000 drinks. José Cuervo Month featured Cuervo "shot girls" on hand every Friday evening. Another time, staff members were divided into two service teams for a month-long competition pitting the Sauza Conmemorativo team against the Cuervo Gold team. Guests get caught up in the staff's enthusiasm and everybody has a great time. At the end of a month guests shout out, "What's next month's theme?"

Training, Training, Training

"We carry about 50 different tequilas," says Barragato. "Most people new to our restaurant order a Cozyman Sampler: five different frozen Margaritas are served in 4-ounce portions positioned on a wood reproduction of a Mayan temple." Each Margarita has a different color and contrasting swizzle sticks. According to Barragato, at times it seems the entire bar, along with guests at nearby tables, are all asking for a Sampler.

"Then they look very carefully at our Margarita and sipping-tequila drink list, to experiment with something new. This is where intensive staff training pays off and gives waiters and bartenders the confidence to fully describe the tequilas under consideration and make intelligent suggestions."

Not only does Cozymel conduct its own training regimen, but every two months a supplier representative will give a 1-1/2 hour seminar on the tequilas that supplier handles.

"The key for us is staff training," says Barragato. "We have to be the tequila experts even if some staff members had never tasted sipping tequila before joining us. Just as important as location, location, location is training, training, training."

21 Beach Party

WITH EIGHT locations near the ocean at various Southern California beach communities, Hennessey's Taverns cater to a young clientele who want fun food and fun drinks. For many customers, the trip home is a short walk or cab ride. For those driving, the menu suggests: "Keep the luck of the Irish with you. Don't drink and drive," or, "If you've had a wee too much, we'll arrange for a cab."

Bloody Marys are big on summer weekend mornings, until about 2 p.m., when bartenders begin to hear calls for beer, vodka and, increasingly, tequila and rum concoctions.

Specialty Drinks

"We serve a slew of rum specialty drinks," says bartender Craig Mitchell at the Hermosa Beach location. "*Rum Punch* has one ounce of rum, one-half ounce amaretto, cranberry and pineapple juice. *Blue Sky* has one ounce of Parrot Bay Rum, one-half ounce blue curaçao, and pineapple juice, and Coco Lopez. *Brass Monkey* has one-half shot of vodka, one-half shot of rum and orange juice. *White Jamaican* has one ounce of Whalers Rum, one-half ounce Kahlua and half-and-half. Very popular is our *Dr. Pepper.* In a shot glass, we pour equal portions of rum and amaretto and drop the shot glass and all into a tall glass half filled with beer." Margaritas are sold in "buckets" (eight-ounce rock glasses), and the tequilas of choice are Cuervo Gold, Cuervo 1800, Tres Generaciones and Sauza Conmemorativo.

Drink specials change seasonally. Beverage manager Mike Gerber's Spring Spirits (1999) were:

Sour Apple Martini – DeKuyper Apple Pucker Schnapps, Skyy Vodka, splash of triple sec, chilled and shaken. Served up.

Ultimate Margarita – Sauza Conmemorativo Añejo Tequila, Tuaca Liqueur, sweet-and-sour mix. Built on the rocks.

Spring Break – Captain Morgan Spiced Rum, Parrot Bay Rum, cranberry juice and 7-Up.

Red Headed Teaser – Jagermeister, Peach Schnapps, cranberry juice, shaken and served up.

Mudslide Shooter – Kahlua, Carolan's Irish Cream and vodka, shaken and served up.

Simple Food and Special Dinners

Breakfast, lunch and dinner menus are filled with simple food items at reasonable prices. An unusual offering that is very popular is the Gourmet Burger Sampler — four mini-burgers with the most popular toppings: cheese, mushroom, guacamole and barbecue sauce with bacon for $5.95. The most expensive item on the regular menu is a 12-ounce New York steak or a filet mignon at $11.95.

To add some spice to beach life there are occasional dinner events such as a Clos Du Bois Wine Dinner held in June that attracts over 70 customers at $29.95 per head. Clos Du Bois Sauvignon Blanc Sonoma was recently served with mixed baby field greens with pear, apple and veal sausage in a mango/honey-mustard dressing.

Chef Steve Matthews then prepared lobster ravioli with sautéed spinach in a light vanilla bean cream sauce, accompanied by Clos Du Bois Chardonnay Alexander Valley, followed by Southwest mesquite-spiced pork tenderloin with caramelized onion and tomato, matched with Clos Du Bois Pinot Noir Sonoma. Dessert was blackberry-infused chocolate bread pudding with Tahitian crème Anglaise, paired with Clos Du Bois Cabernet Sauvignon Alexander Valley.

"Our customers are at the beaches to have a good time and forget the Monday-to-Friday work rituals," says Paul Hennessey. "Most of the time it means kicking back with a few friends and enjoying some drinks along with casual food. When they want something more, we pamper them with a superb special dinner at a reasonable price."

22 Live Entertainment Packs 'em in

PEOPLE WALKING towards the beach along Pier Avenue in Hermosa Beach, California, frequently postpone their date with the sun to duck into The Lighthouse Cafe. The blaring sounds of live jazz or reggae or funk have been an irresistible lure for over 50 years.

"The best Bloody Marys in the South Bay" and specially priced Whaler's Hurricanes, drafts, wines and well drinks generally keep them lingering for the rest of the set.

Owner Paul Hennessey, who also owns Hennessey's Taverns, says the cafe draws an older crowd than the taverns. "Live entertainment is the key — jazz groups at 11 a.m. on weekends, karoake 'Singing with the Hits' on Mondays, Tuesday nights for calypso and reggae, Sunset Jazz Concerts from 5 p.m. to 8 p.m. every Wednesday, Comedy Shoot-outs on Thursdays and Friday Funk Nights."

A large selection of hand-tossed pizzas is offered at $5.95 ($2 each on Mondays and Fridays until 9 p.m.). Fish tacos are $1 on Tuesdays until 10 p.m., steak or salmon filet dinner for $9.95 on Wednesdays. On Thursdays, it's 10-cent wings until 9 p.m.

Many regulars purchase an annual Lighthouse V.I.P. Gold Card Membership. This provides free admission on designated nights, Members-Only parties, complimentary cocktail parties, valuable discounts and front-of-the-line privileges.

"This is another way to show our regular customers that we love them, even when the summer influx can be intimidating," says Hennessey. "It keeps them coming back, in season and out of season."

Snug as an Irish Pub

23

FIRST THERE was a wave of Irish immigrants coming to America, now it's a wave of Irish pubs. In 1995, Chris Martin and Rory Connolly, both from Dublin, opened a pub in San Francisco and called it The Bank of Ireland. They soon heard from lawyers and judiciously changed the name to The Irish Bank. The intent remained the same: "you can deposit your money with us and we'll pay you back with an unforgettable Irish experience."

And that they do. On entering the pub it is truly as if you were on a lane in one of Ireland's small towns. There is a grocery storefront on one wall, with a window filled with actual products offered for sale in the early 1900s. Elsewhere is Connolly's Post Office (Rory's grandmother was a postmaster), with a front window showcasing the goods, aside from stamps, that were for sale.

An antique, old-world style bar serves a keg of Guinness every few hours and is reputed to offer an exceptional Irish coffee, although the Buena Vista might quarrel about that. "If it's an Irish spirit that's available in America, we've got it," adds Martin.

A True Taste of Ireland

"We set an authentic tone, with our vast array of photos of the Irish people and places and our antique collection," says Connolly, "but it's the people who have adopted The Irish Bank as their pub that have given us our personality."

And what a personality! Located on Mark Lane, a secluded block off Bush Street, the restaurant hosts a three-day "blockfest" to celebrate Saint Patrick's

Day and follows up on May 22 with a celebration of Sam Bloom's Day — a paean to James Joyce. The famed author's favorite culinary delights are prepared and customers order two pints, generally Guinness, and place one of them on "Joyce's casket." After emptying the first pint, they nimbly retrieve the second one from atop the casket and continue an extended celebration.

Those of a literary bent, and there are many, dress as James Joyce and his peers might have done and, after reciting some of Joyce's writings, begin a literary pub crawl. The most hardy wind up back at The Irish Bank for a final pint. Nobody drives. I don't know if I'd want to be riding a trolley with this group that night, though.

A Snug

In Ireland many pubs will contain a "snug," a totally private booth for two to six people to get away from the world . . . for whatever reason they might want to do this. The Irish Bank has a snug. In a previous life it was a confessional in a Connemara church. In San Francisco, the interior has been gutted and a table and four seats are in the place of the kneelers and priest's cubicle. The curtains are in place and a hatch has been cut into what had been the priest's door. This enables a server to pass through drinks and food when a tinkling bell alerts them that service is requested. It's very popular.

Time For New York

After four very successful years, it was time to expand and accept the challenge of New York. "There are almost as many Irish pubs in New York City as there are in the all of Ireland," says Martin. And some of the pub owners are good friends who encouraged them to bring their brand of pub to Manhattan.

Keeping the San Francisco pub open, the pair opened The Irish Bank at the end of 1999 in Manhattan, on Fifth Avenue between 32nd and 33rd Streets. While not a clone of the West Coast operation, the same elements make up the new pub, including a snug. It's not another confessional, though. A corner abutting one end of the bar has been closed off and will seat up to six. A hatch opens to the bar when food or drink is desired.

"Our kitchen is open until midnight, sometimes later," says Martin, "and our signature food special, *Lobster Shepherd's Pie,* is so popular that people fear we may eat the lobsters into extinction."

What sets The Irish Bank apart from most Irish pubs in America is that, for a few hours, guests feel that they are actually in Ireland. And they can revisit often on what they have saved on airfare.

Part Five

People come to The Roxy for entertainment. We don't believe entertainment should pause when they come to the bar. If bartenders just take orders, they're costing the club money.
— Scott Young

We have entered a new age of the celebrity bartender, an age when cocktail bartending, for women as well as men, is achieving the same kind of professional status that American chefs have fought so hard to achieve in the kitchen.
— Dale DeGroff

It's the Cheers *syndrome that drives today's bar business. People want to be recognized and they want to feel at home in their bar of choice. Bartenders are critical to making sure that guests feel welcome.*
— Blake Donaldson

Every bottle has a story and our bartenders have to know that story. Then they can bring the savvy customer to another level which will keep that customer coming back, often with friends.
— Michael Waterhouse

The da Vinci of Drink

24

"IN NEW YORK, more than any place else, life takes place in the restaurants and saloons," says Dale DeGroff. "It may not appeal to everyone. But to some of us, as we stand shoulder to shoulder with one foot on the big brass rail, these are indeed the best of times."

In that spirit of camaraderie, he reintroduced the classic cocktails of the past 100 years at the redesigned Rainbow Room, atop the RCA building in New York's Rockefeller Center, in 1987.

The Classic Cocktails

"I researched back to 1850 for original recipes of cocktails no longer being served," he recalls. "From 1850 to 1915, some amazing drinks were being offered, before Prohibition changed the rules."

After "the grand experiment," the classics were martinis, Manhattans, old fashioneds, Rob Roys, stingers, sidecars and alexanders. Forgotten were cobblers, juleps, punches, flips and slings.

Then, in the '70s and '80s, it became fashionable to drink white wine or Perrier. Near the end of the '80s, the swing back to martinis and other classic cocktails began. Many give credit for this resurgence to DeGroff's vision of introducing a new generation to these drinks, made properly and served with flair.

These cocktails were truly "classic." There were no designer ice cubes to fill up the glass to make an ounce-and-a-half pour look humongous.

"Ice pellets melt quickly, resulting in a watered-down drink, not something that will make your bar memorable. Solid 1-1/4-inch ice cubes are called for, with the bartender cracking the ice cubes for drinks requiring cracked ice," DeGroff says.

Since he used only fresh juices, DeGroff had to change the proportions in many drink recipes, employing simple syrup to balance the acidity of the fruit. He trained his bartenders to measure drink ingredients as accurately as chefs measure the ingredients in the dishes they prepare.

The Celebrity Bartender

"We have entered a new age of the celebrity bartender, an age when cocktail bartending, for women as well as men, is achieving the same kind of professional status that American chefs have fought so hard to achieve in the kitchen," DeGroff states emphatically.

"At the Rainbow Room, I asked my 12 bartenders to work like chefs," he explains, "and know their condiments, spices, liquor products and juices, to understand what ingredients taste like and how they combine. Most importantly, they were asked to study and follow the recipes I had developed.

"Whatever the hell you want to be, while you're behind the bar you might as well know everything there is to know about it," he would tell careerists as well as aspiring actors and those tending bar while continuing their college studies. "You might as well know everything because that's the way your life should be anyway."

This was driven home to DeGroff when he was a five-year veteran bartender making a sidecar for a guest at the Hotel Bel Air in Los Angeles. Another guest at the bar said, "I bet you think you made that right, don't you?" He then explained the importance of Cointreau over triple sec, the proper glass to use and how to rim it with sugar. "He was a respected bartender at another L.A. hotel, L'Ermitage," says DeGroff, "and I realized that I didn't know a damned thing about making a proper drink."

Bartenders working for him today know how to make a proper drink. They know how, and when, to flame an orange peel before dropping it into a drink. They know how to improvise when a guest asks for "something new."

Since the mid-'90s, one "something new" has been Cachaca, the Brazilian sugar cane spirit. *Caipirinha* is on the drink list at The Blackbird Bar and Restaurant in New York City, where DeGroff currently presides as beverage manager. This national drink of Brazil is made with Cachaca, simple syrup and muddled limes.

A Sampler of DeGroff's Recipes

Ritz — 1/2 oz. Cognac, 1/2 oz. Cointreau, 1/4 oz. maraschino liqueur, 1/4 oz. fresh lemon juice. Shake with ice and strain into a large martini glass. Top with about 5 oz. Champagne and garnish with a flaming orange peel.

Caipirinha — 2 oz. Cachaca, 1 ounce simple syrup, 1/2 lime quartered. Place lime quarters in the bottom of mixing glass, add simple syrup and muddle, extracting the juice and the oil in the skin from the lime quarters. Chill a rocks glass with cracked ice. Add Cachaca to the mixture in the mixing glass, dump in the ice and shake well. Pour the entire contents of the mixing glass into the chilled rocks glass and serve.

Coffee Cocktail, a variation on the brandy flip — 1-1/2 oz. V.S. Cognac, 1-1/2 oz. 10-year-old Tawny Port wine, one teaspoon sugar, one egg yolk. Shake well and strain into a stemmed Port glass.

Sazerac — Two dashes Peychauds bitters, 2 dashes Angostura bitters, 1 oz. rye whiskey, 1 oz. VS Cognac, splash of Ricard or Herbsaint, 1/4 oz. simple syrup or 1 teaspoon bar sugar. Chill one rocks glass while preparing the drink in the other. Splash the Ricard into the second glass and swirl, then pour it out. Add all other ingredients, stir with ice cubes to chill and strain into the pre-chilled rocks glass and garnish with a lemon peel.

"When this drink was invented, it was probably named for the most popular Cognac of that time, Sazerac de Forge et Fils. As American taste changed to rye whiskey drinks, this became a rye cocktail and, later, a bourbon-based cocktail," DeGroff says. "I have my own twist — a mix of Cognac and rye."

The Flame of Love Martini — One part sherry, six parts vodka, stirred . . . simple enough so far. But the creator, Chasen's bartender Pepe Ruiz, was responding to a challenge by Dean Martin to create a "new" martini. He peeled an entire orange into nine or ten strips. Lighting a wooden match and holding it above the glass, he pinched each peel into the flame, oily skin side toward the flame, reserving one peel. He then poured the drink into the glass over the drops of orange zest and repeated the spectacle with the last strip of peel, dropping the fired-up peel into the drink. DeGroff and his bartenders duplicate this feat, but shy away from using all of the peels from a single orange for only one drink.

Millennium Cocktail — Courvoisier Millennium Cognac, pineapple juice, orange curaçao and Angostura bitters. Created by Dale DeGroff.

At this writing, late 1999, you can find Dale DeGroff at the Windows On The World or you can visit him at his Web site: www.kingcocktail.com.

To get your conversation off on the right foot, ask him to comment on George Jean Nathan's line: "I only drink to make other people interesting."

25

It Takes a Flair

"PERFORMANCE bartending taken to the extreme," says Scott Young, "is what I present behind the bar at The Roxy and in the courses that I teach around the world. I haven't met a customer yet, who doesn't enjoy being entertained."

As a beginning bartender in Vancouver, Young was aware that the best bartenders in that city worked at The Roxy, a 300-seat club with four bars and performances by live bands. Every bartender was adept at performance bartending and there was no turnover.

"If I was ever going to get a job at The Roxy," he remembers, "I would have to not only learn the skills of performance bartending but become outstanding at it."

Practice Makes Perfect

A course he took didn't do much for him, so he and another bartender, Colin Bannon, practiced for six weeks in the backyard of his mother's house, dropping more than a few bottles on the forgiving lawn.

Now confident in their skills, they entered a local contest and placed third. This caught the attention of Vance Campbell, director of operations for The Roxy and, when an opening for a bartender arose six months later, he quickly hired Young.

"I knew Scott for a couple of years before I hired him and respected him as a person intent on improving himself and as a professional behind the bar. But I had no opening for him," says Campbell today.

"When I suddenly had an opening (the first in the three years since The Roxy opened), I quickly grabbed him."

Young says his greeting the first day on the job was right to the point. "Let's see what you've got, Kid," said one of the veteran bartenders as, standing on top of the bar, he flipped a bottle to Young. He knew what to do and quickly became part of the team.

Young also knew that getting this job didn't mean he could now rest on his laurels. *Au contraire.* Most of his free time was spent watching and learning from his teammates, especially Andy MacBeth and Sasha Poceckovic. Then, he and Bannon practiced what they had seen . . . over and over. Until they knew a trick cold, they wouldn't perform it on the job.

Practice had two dimensions. The technical side encompassed moving slowly to fully evaluate every step and every motion, then turning the music up, singing and dancing as the flow of the trick is established. After this was mastered, creativity was given free rein to develop the passion and style that would bring the bar crowd alive and pull table-sitters off their stools and over to the bar.

People Want to be Entertained

"People come to The Roxy for entertainment," Young says. "We don't believe entertainment should pause when they come to the bar. If bartenders just take orders, they're costing the club money."

Think about this: The Roxy bartenders put on a dazzling show mixing cocktails. Half of their beverage sales are liquor sales, with a lot of bottles of Cristal Champagne ordered by some of their more affluent customers. But as talented as these bartenders are, service comes first.

"Our bartenders can perform at any time as long as people are served promptly. This is not a circus where people have to hail a beer vendor," says Campbell. "Scott is excellent at performing with no loss of speed in delivering the drink to his customer. Others may have to leave the performing to slow times at the bar. Each bartender develops his own pace."

Young echoes this imperative when he says, "Know when, and when not, to use the tricks. The number one job of a bartender is to increase sales revenue. Be entertaining. Be fast. But if you can't do a trick without spilling, it's not worth doing."

He stresses using no-risk moves that work whether its busy or slow, with no spillage and no waiting. "Flip bottles half filled with juice, rather than the liquor bottles," he adds. "Spilling liquor is a no-no."

Shtick Increases Checks

Once customers are caught up in the imagery, they'll respond readily to, "I've got something you're going to love." They do love what Young makes for them, and check averages do rise.

Young treats his bar as a house party, opening the door to interaction with his customers. When it's slow, he'll invite a customer behind the bar to make his or her own drink. When others clamor for their chance behind the bar, he'll smile and say, "Hey, come back later," or ". . . the next time you're in." Always give people a reason to come back.

After two years on the job at The Roxy, Young had many requests to teach performance bartending to other bartenders. He developed a short course curriculum and formed a company, Bar Smart, to put on training seminars anywhere in the world. During his time off, Young and his staff put on a number of seminars in Vancouver and nearby venues, learning what worked and eventually producing a four-video training course from which individual bartenders can train themselves.

"I believe strongly in what Scott and his team are doing," says Vance Campbell. "We have enough highly trained performance bartenders in all of our venues that I can pull replacements for The Roxy when Scott and his team have training dates. In our early days, a guy from Malta was so impressed with Andy MacBeth and Sasha Poceckovic that he hired them to teach their skills and put on exhibitions in Malta. They were gone for almost three months that summer."

If you'd like to talk to Scott Young about having Bar Smart train your bartenders or if you want information about their video training course, you can reach him at (604) 879-1036 or check his Web site: www.extremebartending.com.

— Advice From Scott Young —

- If you don't entertain your customers, someone else will.
- If you're going to serve it, serve it with style.
- When tossing a bottle, mixer, straw or stirrer, the higher you throw it the longer you have to get your other hand in position to catch it.
- Pause after every action before moving on to the next action.
- When catching something, create a cushion. Don't be like the football player who drops the perfect pass because it bounces off his chest.
- Flip juice, not alcohol.
- Show your customers you care about them by suggesting new drinks that they'll like. Ask them if they like drinks creamy, refreshing, sweet or tart, and produce accordingly.
- Great bartenders do more than take orders.
- Ask, "Do you want a lime with that?" as you throw a lime in the air so that it lands in the drink glass held behind your back with your other hand. If the guest says yes while the lime is in the air, present the drink with lime. If he or she says no, let the lime keep sailing and quickly present the glass sans lime, smiling and saying, "I don't like limes either."
- Have fun, but take it seriously.
- Don't take yourself too seriously.

Creating Room Energy

26

"IT'S THE CHEERS Syndrome that drives today's bar business," says Blake Donaldson, beverage director for Michi Restaurant & Bar in Manhattan Beach, California. "People want to go out to mingle, to have fun. They want to be recognized and they want to feel at home in their bar of choice. Bartenders are critical to making sure the guest feels welcome."

Donaldson believes that "room energy" is necessary to generate perpetual business. Bartenders continually work the room to make everybody feel that they are guests at a very "in" party. He encourages his bartenders to introduce themselves to every guest approaching the bar. On Thursdays, Fridays and Saturdays, when the bar is packed with L.A.'s "hippest crowd" and sound level is high, they'll shout their hellos.

Donaldson's credo is that he's not selling food and drink, he's selling satisfaction.

"Who wants a *Stoplight?*" shouts Donaldson, and the crescendo of "I dos" focuses all eyes on him as he sets up two six-ounce martini glasses side by side and balances a third on top. In one ice-filled mixing glass he prepares a green-colored martini cocktail, in a second he prepares a yellow-colored martini cocktail and in a third he prepares a red-colored martini cocktail.

Stacking one mixing glass inside another, he then grasps the three glasses around the middle with one hand, and positions them horizontally above the stacked martini glasses so the red drink flows into one glass as the yellow and green drinks simultaneously flow, separately, into the other two glasses. To the roar of the crowd he then places each of the glasses in front of the first three people he targeted for this round's entertainment.

"Michi opened in 1996 as a high-end 'Pacific Fusion' restaurant with a fun Martini Bar within its portals. Michi, our renowned chef, won immediate plaudits from reviewers and diners alike. The dining room is always busy," he says. "and our Martini Bar has also been a big hit from the beginning. Almost 300 martinis will be sold over a weekend, from a variety of more than 30 that we offer, accounting for 70 percent of our total beverage sales. We have the unusual situation where our revenues are divided equally between food and beverages."

The Traditional Martini

"Traditional martinis are not drinks that most people can consume all evening and still function, one must be careful," Donaldson cautions. "But for the occasional, true martini drinker we use a full glass of ice, add the vodka or gin of choice and a sprinkle of dry vermouth, shake vigorously and let it set for 15 seconds to soften the spirits a little. We strain it into a six-ounce martini glass and garnish with three olives slid onto a blue pick. There is always a remainder in the mixing glass which we pour into a small decanter and place beside the drink as a 'dividend.'"

When a twist is requested, bartenders cut a complete circle of peel off the lemon, twist it and pull it taut over the drink, ring the glass and then drop it into the martini. "It's the oil of the lemon that adds the essence," explains Donaldson. "You must twist the peel to extract this oil, hence a 'twist.' The romance of the martini lies in the personal nature of me preparing you a special cocktail, individually mixed just for you. Shaken or stirred? I prefer shaken!"

Cocktail Martinis

"Today's new craze for martinis is all about variety," Donaldson continues. "And what gives martinis 'legs' are the different products I have to choose from to concoct a tasty cocktail for my guest. I now have creative license to do anything I want, pour it into a martini glass and call it a *Lemon Drop Martini* or a *Stoplight Martini* . . . whatever. These are very tasty drinks, with less alcohol than the traditional martini, that the average customer can enjoy over an evening without going overboard."

To make a Lemon Drop Martini: Place two lemon wedges in a mixing glass and pound with a mulling mallet. Add three parts vodka, two parts low-alcohol triple sec and a generous amount of lemonade. In a glass rimmed with sugar place a fresh, stretched lemon strip and then fill with the elixir.

To make Donaldson's Stoplight Martini: In each of three mixing glasses pour three parts vodka and two parts triple sec. Prepare and add a melon ball to one glass, a fuzzy navel to a second glass and cranberry juice with a squeeze of lemon to the third glass. Shake each well and proceed as previously described.

Beverages are not neglected on the restaurant side of Michi's. The wine list features 100 wines, mostly from California, with 20 available by the glass. Donaldson has not yet developed a wine-based martini, but who knows what the millennium might bring? Cheers to all!

You can visit Black Donaldson on his Web site: www.mrmartini.com.

27 Bartenders are a Rare Resource

"IN THE PAST 10 years I've consulted for, and opened, over 40 bars," says Michael Waterhouse. "Many of them are currently doing very well." We have to listen to a man with that track record.

"In Manhattan, bartending is not seen as a profession but as a way station while pursuing careers as actors, writers and other creative endeavors," Waterhouse continues. "This poses a challenge for operators in a city where bar customers are far more educated about wines and spirits than most bartenders. Frequently, I will hire people with outgoing personalities who may have no bar experience but show an eagerness to learn." New hires and veterans alike will participate in ongoing, 30-minute training sessions every week or two.

"Every bottle has a story and our bartenders have to know that story," says Waterhouse. "Then they can bring the savvy customer to another level which will keep that customer coming back, often with friends."

Dylan's, an upscale Tribeca bar with room for 85 people, was opened by Waterhouse and his partner, John Mautone, in September 1999. Next door they opened Laight Street, a seafood restaurant seating 125. One kitchen serves both operations.

"The bar business has gone from quantity to quality," Waterhouse says. "We serve every drink with a flair. When a vintage Port is opened, it is immediately decanted carefully, leaving its sediment in the bottle, which is then rinsed. The sediment-free Port is then returned to its original bottle for pouring."

Five red wines and five white wines are offered by the glass, as well as 50 half bottles priced from $15 to $100. Pinot noirs and red zinfandels are well represented on the wine list. Eight draft beers, with a diversity of style, and a bottle list from Budweiser to high-end Belgian ales highlights the beer offerings.

Old-Fashioned Cocktail List

"We're starting with Armagnacs and Calvados, as well as Cognacs, 30 single malt Scotches and 40 classic cocktails, including ones rarely found in New York — Ramos fizz, mint julep, sidecar, for instance," says Waterhouse.

"It's imperative that all bartenders consistently prepare these drinks properly. Each drink should taste the same no matter who prepares it."

High staff turnover would make this impossible. Waterhouse believes the staff should be treated as professionals. What does this mean? "We pay above the going scale and raise hourly pay with longevity. We treat everybody with respect and invite their suggestions," he says. "If they need special time off, we do our best to accommodate them. We demand a lot but we also give a lot. A happy staff emits the vibes that bring customers back."

Food Grazing

People at bars often want something light to eat. The Laight Street restaurant menu offers half portions of many of its dishes. A bar menu of these dishes allows a group to pick and choose a variety of foods that are then shared. Servers suggest different half bottles of wine that would be particularly good with various foods selected.

Food is served as prepared and guests comfortably eat as much, or as little, as they want.

"After nine years as beverage director for the Myriad Restaurant Group," Waterhouse adds, "I am eager to put what I learned from that great experience into building another great restaurant enterprise."

28 Performance Bartending

PERFORMANCE bartending was a fixture in Canadian clubs for years before Tom Cruise dazzled young adults in *Cocktail,* the movie.

Vance Campbell, director of operations for Granville Enterprises, remembers employing performance bartenders in clubs he ran in Alberta as early as 1985.

When business partner, Blaine Culling, of Granville Entertainment, purchased a club in downtown Vancouver, British Columbia, they quickly decided to close for extensive remodeling.

"We reopened it in June 1988 as The Roxy, with a staff of performance bartenders and two house bands," remembers Campbell. "It was an immediate, huge hit and business has increased every year, despite an economy in British Columbia that has been in the tank for the past five or six years."

Every bartender was adept at tossing bottles, shakers, straws and garnishes. The bottles almost always contained juices and mixes, seldom liquor. Spilling liquor has always been a no-no.

"A drink is a drink is a drink," says Campbell. "The big bucks come from the shtick. Give the customers a show that they can't get someplace else and they'll stay in your place and keep coming back."

High Energy Level Vital

After operating clubs for 15 years in neighboring Alberta, Campbell knew that a high energy level was important to success. House bands playing cover tunes from the '70s and '80s kept things lively, with DJs taking over during breaks.

"We raised the heights of our tables, in banquettes and on the floor, with stools replacing chairs. It introduced a feel of being with-it, rather than relaxing at a table as an observer," he says.

The razzle-dazzle was important to attract a milling crowd to the bar since it had only been about 10 years that British Columbia law allowed customers to be served at the bar and many were quite comfortable waiting for service at their tables. Now 90 percent of beverage sales are at the four bars.

"Fortunately, I had two men who were highly skilled performance bartenders, Andy MacBeth and Sasha Poceckovic," says Campbell. "They taught themselves through practice, practice and more practice, inventing moves and working on them until they were confident enough to introduce them on the job. This inspired the rest of the staff, who worked hard to keep up."

The four bars were crowded every night, customers laughing and bantering with the bartenders and coming back with friends to show off "their place."

All of The Roxy bartenders had to learn how to be performance bartenders without spilling any alcohol. Not only would this make management unhappy, it could cost all the bartenders money.

Our Front Line Is Our Bottom Line

From day one Campbell and Culling paid daily cash bonuses to each pair of bartenders whose sales exceeded the quota for their bar (two bartenders and one porter at each bar and one runner serving all four bars). At the end of the week, if the p.c. (pouring costs) didn't come in at the level the staff knew management wanted, no bartender received a bonus for the following week.

Over the years this would happen about 20 percent of the time. Peer pressure keeps everybody performing optimally.

"Our front line is our bottom line," Campbell says fervently. "Everybody interfacing with a customer has to make a good impression on that customer. We want that customer to have a good time, to tell his or her friends and to come back. To that end we spoil our staff rotten . . . gladly. From two-and-a-half to three percent of our gross sales is given out in staff bonuses and incentives."

Staff turnover is virtually nil. Bartender Scott Young (whom you met in chapter 25) had to wait a couple of years before an opening allowed him to be hired in 1991. He's still there, as are MacBeth and Poceckovic.

Dr. Strangelove has been the back-of-the-week house band since 1992, and Joe's Garage has played the first three nights of the week since 1997, following The Real McCoys who played for about 8 years.

The Roxy draws mostly a young crowd, ages 19 (the legal age in British Columbia) through 25, plus a slightly older group who are too fond of its camaraderie to give it up.

Flair at the Bar Increases Profits

About half of the beverage sales are high profit liquor, with beer right behind, and some demand for ciders and coolers. Oh, yes, bottles of Champagne account for one percent of all beverage sales. Enough sports figures stop in to put a major dent in the stock of Cristal Champagne.

"With the success of The Roxy and the decision of the city to encourage an 'Entertainment Zone' in the heart of downtown Vancouver, we spread our wings," Campbell says. "In 1992, we took over the management of The Vogue, a venerable vaudeville theater that now features live band concerts as well as an occasional touring play, most recently, *Rent.*"

Foghorn's Roadhouse, a chicken restaurant with a long stand-up bar was opened in 1994, followed two years later by the purchase and $3-million renovation of the Hotel Dakota, a 100-room boutique hotel offering luxury at affordable prices. Its slogan is: "This is not the Holiday Inn."

You don't have to be told that when you enter the hotel's BaBalu Tapas Lounge, designed to remind you of a has-been Cuban casino. Drawing a 25- to 40-year-old crowd, cigars and martinis are very big. Pop Latin and Contemporary bands play Sunday through Thursday, and a DJ plays a Latin/Contemporary mix of music on weekends.

Another hotel spot is Fred's Tavern, a video and sports bar in the best American tradition. It attracts a 25- to 30-year-old group.

Do you get the feeling you should be visiting Vancouver?

Tempt Your Guests with a Pre-Taste

29

A HOT SPOT for athletes and celebrities, New York's Angelo and Maxie's Steak House, fills their 265 seats 4,000 to 5,000 times a week. And it ain't just steaks that pack them in. Twenty service people are on the floor of the main dining room every night, along with a sommelier. Virtually every table orders wine with dinner, and after dinner it's not unusual to see full bottles of Port on many tables. Ten of the 12 Ports offered can be served by the glass and a half bottle of vintage Port is also available.

Wall Street regulars, celebrities and athletes generally head through the dining room to the back and enter Havana Rick's, a cigar bar restaurant-within-the-restaurant seating 45, with another 10 seats at it's bar. Kevin Carrigan presides behind the bar on Wednesday, Thursday and Saturday nights and is justly famous for his *White Chocolate Martini* – four ounces of Stoli Vanil mixed with two ounces of white crème de cacao and served in a large martini glass previously dipped into warm melted white chocolate. But this bar is about more than martinis.

The Pre-Taste Test

"When people come through the door to Havana Rick's, they immediately see a wall of small-batch bourbons and single malt Scotches," says Carrigan, who has been with the restaurant since its opening on Halloween in 1996. "When a guest at the bar ponders over what to order, I'll pour a small taste of Baker's small-batch bourbon into a Cognac snifter and suggest he or she try it. Frequently I then hear, 'I hate bourbon but I like this.' Seldom are guests exposed to the best of a product and just don't know of the subtlety and nuances trapped in an unopened bottle of fine spirits."

Similarly, when a guest orders a particular brand of single malt Scotch, he will often pour a small taste of another malt that might be appreciated. Single malt drinkers are like serious wine drinkers in that they are adventurous and open to new taste experiences. It's part of the fun. A determined fan of Laphroiag 10 year old, and Laphroiag drinkers are all determined, is often pleasantly amazed at the dramatic difference of the 15-year-old Laphroiag, "You'll know it's an Islay malt, but it is considerably less briny than it's 10-year-old brother," he says.

Wine drinkers will often receive a small taste of what they ordered, along with a: "See if you really like this or would want to try something else," from Carrigan. The guest may have had that same wine with a meal and enjoyed it very much. Taken without food, the wine will not taste the same and he wants to give the guest an opportunity to notice this and change to a more appropriate choice if he or she desires.

The biggest selling cocktail is the Cosmopolitan made with Absolut Citron. For straight martinis the call is for Belvedere, Ketel One and Grey Goose. Remy Louis XIII gets enough calls, at $150 for 2-1/4 ounces, to empty a 1.5 liter bottle every month.

A Woman-Friendly Atmosphere

"Many women are very comfortable in this room," says restaurant manager Linda Sondik. "Though many of the 800 to 1,000 cigars sold weekly in the restaurant are lit up in the cigar bar, state-of-the-art ventilation clears smoke almost immediately. Some women get in the spirit of the room and light up a cigar, but most are content to have a drink and perhaps make new friends. We don't have a 'boy's club' atmosphere. It's relaxed and friendly — conducive to people having a non-threatening time and enjoying themselves."

Professionalism is Important

"Keeping a high energy level in the room is the mark of a professional bartender," Carrigan asserts. "Never just stand there waiting for something to happen. When it isn't busy, move about the bar doing something. I have a glass washer at the bar and instruct the floor staff to bring all dirty glasses to the bar as they clear them from the tables. It doesn't take long to wash three or four glasses, polish them with a soft cloth and place gleaming glassware in front of a guest. It also makes my job easier because polished glasses, when stacked, separate as effortlessly as a silk stocking from a powdered leg."

30 Turning Slow Times into Show Times... It's Magic!

MAGICAL bartenders pull out their bag of tricks when the pace slows down and people at the bar are not engrossed in conversations with friends.

Doc Eason, one of the most famous "magical" bartenders in America works a few nights a week at the Tower Club in Aspen, Colorado. It's typical for customers, sometimes with spouses and children, to become so mesmerized that they'll order some food and a few more drinks over a few hours. Often they had planned on eating someplace else, but were having so much fun they just stayed put and had a ball. "That's the name of the game. Keep your customers entertained and they'll spend their money with you instead of the competition," says Louis Melamed, who has taught simple magic tricks to thousands of bartenders.

"You don't have to master sleight-of-hand to entertain your bar customers with intriguing illusions. Many tricks are self-working, requiring no skill to perform. The key is to start with easy-to-learn tricks that can be set up and performed quickly."

Some of the "anyone can perform them" tricks that Melamed teaches are:

The floating glass — While the bartender pours a drink he or she lets go of the glass and it remains suspended in mid-air while the drink continues to be poured.

The bendable spoon — A spoon appears to be bent completely in half, yet when the bartender opens a hand, the spoon is seen straight and untouched.

The floating match — A match is removed from a matchbook and placed on top of a playing card and instantly floats above the card in mid-air.

Aldini rising card — A chosen card rises out of a deck of cards sitting in a glass.

Princess card trick — The bartender shows a fan of five cards and asks everyone to think of one of the five cards and write it down. Everyone chooses the same card.

D'lites — A ball of light appears at the fingertips of the bartender. The light is passed from hand to hand and then tossed to a waiter across the bar. The waiter passes the light from hand to hand and then tosses it back to the bartender who makes it vanish instantly.

You get the idea. It's easy and requires little practice and no special gifts. What happens when a heckler starts in? Be prepared with good, swift comebacks. "I know how that's done" can be answered with: "So do I! Don't tell anyone." "I've seen that before" gets an: "Okay, then I won't show it to anyone." And a "Hey, how did you do that?" can be answered with: "Very well, thank you." Don't be gulled into doing a trick a second time for the same audience. Say, "If you want to see that again, you'll have to come back another time." Always smiling.

"Don't confuse magic tricks with bar bets and challenges," adds Melamed. "One challenges the customer to try to figure out the secret answer, while the other offers pure entertainment and puts customers in awe. Never reveal how a trick is performed. Leave them guessing and they'll return . . . with friends."

A Magic Trick for You to Try

Write down the number 1089 on a piece of paper and fold it so customers cannot see it. Explain that you have written down a prediction on this piece of paper and ask them to think of any three-digit number using the digits 1 through 9. Each of the three digits has to be different, e.g., 1-2-3. Have the customer reverse the digits, i.e., 3-2-1.

Tell the customer to subtract the smaller number from the larger, e.g., 321-123 = 198.

Now have them reverse the three-digit total, e. g., 891.

Have the customer add the subtraction total to the reverse figure, e. g., 198 + 891 = 1089.

The answer is always 1089. Try it; you'll amaze yourself. Only do it once for your customers. Do not repeat the trick, but please have fun with it.

Louis Melamed gives seminars on using magic in a bar or restaurant setting and manufactures and sells magic tricks designed for use in bars and restaurants through "Tricks on Tap." If you are interested in setting up a seminar for your bartenders or want a catalog of magic tricks, please call 1-800-568-3464 or 651-426-0059. Written correspondence can be sent to: Tricks On Tap, 325 Park Avenue, Mahtomedi, MN 55115-1643. Email: Loudini@aol.com.

Part Six

Fine dining requires fine wine.
— Brian Arbesfeld

One of the pleasures of wine dinners is that you sometimes get wines you'd otherwise never see — older stuff, straight from the winery, and rare stuff . . . "Winemaker's Dinners" let wineries and restaurants show what they do best.
— Dorothy J. Gaiter and John Brecher
"Tastings" Column - The Wall Street Journal, *October 15, 1999*

Our guests have to be adventuresome because we definitely are . . . These [themed] dinners were begun in 1993 to add excitement for our regular customers. They give us an opportunity to serve food and wines that are more interesting and unique than people expect to find in a neighborhood restaurant.
— Les Barnes

We found out the hard way that we have to pay close attention to our scheduling of these affairs. We stay away from July and August, our busiest months, and January and February. We don't schedule an event during national or religious holidays, school closings or vacation times.
— Barry Frommer

It's a mistake to pour generic wines that your servers are embarrassed to name. Offer recognizably good wines that your staff can brag about and price them so that the first glass covers your bottle cost.
— Kevin Zraly

We are in the hospitality business and want all of our guests to feel special. Having brands that they want, which may be difficult to find elsewhere, reinforces the principle that we care.
— Sharon Cooper

While sales of the great classified growths increase every year, there has been a huge demand for wines from the newly developing wine regions worldwide. The coast of Chile, for instance, is a mirror image of California's coast. Because of a lack of government standards, you would be well advised to stick to those wines developed in cooperation with leading French and American winemakers.
— Gil Travalin

31 Zraly on Wine

"WINDOWS ON The World in New York City is the largest seller of wine in the world," says Kevin Zraly, who created the restaurant's opening wine program from scratch in 1976.

"The restaurant, under Chef Michael Lomanica's direction, did over $38 million in 1999 and $5 million of that was wine sales," he adds. "When I first began learning about wine, some thirty years ago, California wines didn't exist in the minds of wine cognoscenti. The bulk of today's sales are of California wines.

"It's the KISS [Keep it simple, sweetheart!] theory at work. In the past you had to study French, German or Italian in order to fully understand what the labels were telling you about the contents of the wine bottle. California labels and wine types are pronounceable and easily understood. And it helps that the quality keeps improving dramatically."

Zraly is presently beverage director of Windows On The World, director of Kevin Zraly's Windows On The World Wine School, author of *The Complete Windows On The World Course* (1,500,000 copies have been sold at this writing) and president of Wine Services International.

Windows On The World Wine School

Zraly personally teaches each session of the eight-week wine course, which attracts 600 students a year. Meeting one evening a week for two hours, the $795 course is quickly sold out. Ninety percent of the participants are consumers. His invitation to you is to come and see what your guests are interested in. It could be a revelation. "I always ask, 'Who drinks more red wine than white wine?'" Zraly says. "Ninety percent raise their hands. Half of these attendees are women and while the average age is about 32, some are as young as 21 and I had an 80-year-old gentleman in a recent class. Twenty percent are from foreign countries, many from France."

A Changing Wine Culture

His point is that wine is touching everybody, all over the country and at every income level. Napa Valley has become the third largest individual tourist destination in the United States, following right behind Disney World and the San Diego Zoo.

Americans are becoming very knowledgeable about wine and expect a greater knowledge from the restaurant staff, as well as from restaurant management. With this knowledge comes resentment when they are met with pomposity and arrogance, and impatience when they are met with ignorance by their servers. A casualty of this increased wine knowledge was Cellars In The Sky, a 36-seat "restaurant-within-a-restaurant" at Windows On The World. For 23 years the chef created an outstanding seven-course meal accompanied by five different wines. There was one sitting at 7:30 p.m., six nights a week.

"While an occasional wine dinner, at a favorite restaurant, will still draw a crowd, not enough people want to do this on a frequent enough basis to fill seats six nights a week," Zraly says. "Another factor was the hour. People don't want to sit down to a three-hour meal at 7:30 p.m., especially if the next day is a workday."

In early 1999, Wild Blue replaced Cellars In The Sky. While still a "restaurant-within-a-restaurant," it now offers anytime-seating with an à la carte menu, 30 wines by the glass and 50 half bottles, perhaps growing to 75 half bottles. With a view of the Statue of Liberty, it attracts about 120 people each night.

Wine Director as Entertainer

Zraly also delivers 50 lectures a year for corporate clients wishing to present a uniquely interesting program at a sales meeting or other corporate event. Ninety percent of the time, a wine dinner custom-designed by Zraly is part of the presentation. At other times a tasting of wines, selected by Zraly, is held.

"At these presentations, and in my classes, I try to bring an understanding of taste and olfactory sensations to each person," he continues. "Wine is highly personal; therefore, it is important to know your own palate and tastes and understand that others might have different reactions to the same wine. In classes, I also teach how to order wine in a restaurant and how to walk into a retail store and select a wine."

What Does This Mean to You?

Zraly feels very strongly that it's a big mistake for servers to automatically present the wine list to a male at a table. Always ask, "Who would like to see our wine list?" If more than one responds in the affirmative, quickly acquire extra lists for all interested parties.

When Joe Baum hired Zraly as wine director of Windows On The World, he advised him: "Keep the prices of wine low and accessible."

Twenty-four years later, Zraly modifies that somewhat. He suggests that restaurateurs carry a large selection of good wines at reasonable prices, a large selection of very good wines at market prices and, depending on the interests of your clientele, a selection of exceptional wines at whatever price you think you can get.

"You know your customers, what they want and what they are comfortable spending," he says. "You, or your wine director, may travel to Europe, to wine areas of the United States or to other wine-producing areas to find boutique wines that your customers would enjoy. You may have a cooling system that keeps red and white wines at optimum temperatures. These costs, as well as the product cost, should be factored into your pricing decisions. The final consideration is, 'will my guests consider this a good value?'"

Wine by the Glass

Zraly has always been an advocate of selling wine by the glass. Serving five ounces in a glass will realistically produce four-and-a-half glasses per bottle (allowing for slight variations by the pourer). "It's a mistake to pour generic wines that your servers are embarrassed to name," he says. "Offer recognizably good wines that your staff can brag about and price them so that the first glass covers your bottle cost (giving you a pouring cost of about 23 percent). You may decide to make some exceptions to this formula; you know your clientele."

In addition to offering many wines by the glass, he suggests a large selection of half bottles. Once very difficult to come by, there is now an abundance of choices. Why? Because many people prefer a bottle of fine wine but do not want to drink a full bottle. Most states don't allow doggy bags for wine. It took winemakers a long time to react to this. That they now have, with gusto, should deliver a message to you.

"An extensive wine-by-the-glass program does not necessarily need a nitrogen system," adds Zraly. "Immediately recork and refrigerate opened bottles, red and white. This should hold the wine well for a couple of days. When re-serving a red, let it sit for a while before pouring. It will soon be at the 58 degrees that is optimal for it. (Consider that most red wines are being served at 70 degrees, not the optimum temperature.)

"For more delicate wines such as pinot noirs and dessert wines you might consider a wine closure or barrier dispenser such as Private Preserve, but these will only be as good as the care with which they are utilized by your staff. Proper execution is important to your bottom line."

A Sample Corporate Program

A Reception/Dinner for 300 at the West Terrace and Delegates Dining Room at the United Nations from 6 p.m. to 10:30 p.m.

— Welcome Reception from 6 p.m. to 7 p.m. —

Beverages: Premium open bar, mixed drinks,
Fortani de France red and white wines, domestic and imported beers,
soft drinks, juices and mineral waters.
Hors D'Oeuvres: Baby artichokes with aioli, Montrachet and fennel in
phyllo; dim sum of chicken, beef and shrimp with scallion soy sauce;
spicy duck empanada; lobster and lemon grass wrapped in rice paper;
ginger curry dipping sauce; shrimp salad with dill and
fennel on endive points; spicy barbecued chicken in corn cups;
potato pancakes with gravlax and honey mustard.

— Seated Dining 7:15 p.m. —

Lobster Risotto with Wehlener Sonnenuhr Reisling '97,
Weingut Max Richter Beringer Chardonnay
Tournedo of Beef on Provençal Vegetable Tart, Potato Straws and
Cabernet Sauce with Santa Rita Reserve '97 Cabernet,
Joseph Drouhin Volnay '96
Fresh Fig and Walnut Tart with Taylor Fladgate 10 year Tawny Port
Coffee and Tea Service

32

Fine Wine... Without Limit

FULL-PAGE ads in *The New York Times* regularly proclaim: "The Cité Prix Fixe Wine Dinner. Where the Food Has No Equal and the Glass Has No Bottom."

The ad copy goes on to announce: "At Cité, we believe fine wine should be celebrated, not rationed. It's a belief we put into practice every night from 8:00 p.m. until closing with our prix fixe wine dinner.

"For $59.95, select three courses from our award-winning menu and, at no extra charge, we'll fill your glass with unlimited quantities of four of the fine wines you see below."

Wine labels from 16 fine wines are shown. Four of these are offered for a three-month period, then a different selection of four is featured for the next three months, and so on. Taittinger Champagne, Clos Duval Cabernet Sauvignon, Robert Mondavi Napa Valley Cabernet Sauvignon and LaBoure-Roi Chablis 1er Cru are some of the wines offered.

"We serve over 2,000 wine dinners a month," says Beverage Manager Mike McCann. Champagne is served before and during appetizers, a choice of one white or two reds with the meal and frequently Champagne with dessert."

Late Night Diners

Additionally, late dining attracts another 500 to 600 guests each month, who will have à la carte dinners, selecting their wines from over 300 selections on Cité's complete wine list.

"Wine dinners account for 35 to 40 percent of the wine consumption in the restaurant," says McCann. "In addition to the four wines served at the wine dinners, three white wines and four red wines are available by the glass."

Almost half of the guests order an after-dinner drink, with the biggest seller being Fonseca Guimaraens 1978 Port. Beaumes de Venise Muscat sells a case of half bottles a month, double that in November and December. Cognac sales are led by XO and VSOP.

Winemaker's Luncheons

Twice a year since 1987, Cité participates in National Wine Week, along with The Post House, Smith & Wollensky, Maloney & Porcelli, The Manhattan Ocean Club, Park Avenue Café and Mrs. Park's Tavern. The restaurants are all members of Alan Stillman's Restaurant Group, one or more of which are located in New York City, Chicago, Washington, D.C., Miami, New Orleans and Las Vegas. Each weekday during lunch, at least eight winery representatives visit guests at their tables, offering three-ounce complimentary tastings of their wines, not all of which are on the current wine list. A different group of wineries is represented each day.

Regulars are quick to make reservations for these weeks, with lunch covers virtually doubling to 2,500 for each week. Most guests fill out the evaluation sheets supplied, giving the restaurant and the wineries valuable input on how well each wine is received by knowledgeable wine drinkers.

The Afternoon Crowd

At other times, not much drinking occurs at lunch. Some wine by the glass and some beer, but the big seller is bottled water. "We sell more water than beer," says McCann. "Late in the afternoon people come in for cocktails and we'll sell a lot of martinis. Our guests expect the traditional martini, not a sweet-tasting concoction served in a martini glass."

While vodka rules, gin martinis get a strong call. Monthly sales average a case each for Beefeater, Bombay Sapphire and Tanqueray. Bombay Gin sells over a case.

Building a Wine Cellar

"FINE DINING requires fine wines," says Brian Arbesfeld, chef/owner of Focaccia Grill in Wantagh, New York. "In less than four years after our opening in 1995, we have grown our table wine selections to over 150, with 12,000 bottles in inventory. That's from an initial offering of 15 whites and 15 reds." Every year since 1996, the restaurant has garnered *Wine Spectator* awards.

There was no instant fix here. "When you buy wines at auction," advises Wine Director Len LoRusso, "you can immediately add prestigious wines to your list but, unless you are a major player, you have no knowledge of how well they have been stored. Sometimes half of the wine could be corked and you won't know about it until a guest complains." Not good for the bottom line; not good for your restaurant's reputation.

"We invest in new wines year after year, buying from knowledgeable wine distributors who buy directly from the wineries. We hold wines off the list until they are ready to be enjoyed," LoRusso adds. "This could be three years or more for some of the complicated reds, and some long-lived California chardonnays can benefit from another year or two of aging."

He stresses the importance of knowing the legal definitions that winemakers live by. This differs from region to region, so examine the labels. California law, for example, mandates that for a wine to be labeled as a varietal (like cabernet sauvignon, zinfandel or merlot), 75 percent of the grapes have to be of that variety. If the label says it's a Napa Valley or Sonoma Valley or any specific appellation, then 85 percent of the grapes have to be grown in that geographical area. If the label carries a vintage year, then 95 percent of the grapes must be harvested in that year.

While this information assures you of the standards met by a particular wine, the skills of the winemaker and the inherent quality of the grapes determine the greatness of an individual wine.

Focaccia offers a selection of meritage wines from California that are quite outstanding while not necessarily conforming to one or more of the above standards. "Some winemakers want the freedom to 'make their own soup' as do their cousins in Bordeaux," says LoRusso. "Varying the proportions of cabernet sauvignon, cabernet franc, merlot and malbec, they bring their unfettered style to the creation of truly fine wines."

He adds that wines from France designated "Appelation Controlée" are produced under strict controls while those designated "Vin de Pays" are generally of lesser quality and not as strictly controlled. Since French wines are more variable from one vintage to another, unlike California wines, it is important to heed the advice of a respected distributor. Oregon wines will also vary by vintage.

LoRusso advises caution with the wines from the Wild Wild West — Chile and Argentina. "The potential for these wines is exciting and some excellent values are available, but the inconsistencies from harvest to harvest are incredible," he shrugs. "There are currently no governmental standards being enforced. On a visit to these regions, I tasted an excellent wine one day and a few days later tasted another bottle proclaiming the same producer, vintage year and varietal, which was undrinkable — not because of poor storage, it was just a bad wine. Today [1999], perhaps 5 percent of South American wines are acceptable by U. S. standards."

When offered wines from these regions ask your supplier for the names of the producers. French and American winemakers of stature are purchasing vineyards in these countries and entering into joint ventures with local producers. They are, or will be, producing wines to their standards, waiting for governmental regulations to come into play.

Special Wine Events

"We are having a special dinner with wines from Spain (or Bordeaux or Portugal), would you like to join us?" In essence this is what Brian Arbesfeld asks the 600 people on his mailing list, six times a year. No mention is made of the food to be served, only the price and the date, generally a Tuesday.

Chef Arbesfeld and Sommelier LoRusso collaborate on the cuisine and wine matchings, serving five to eight courses and five to ten wines. Sometimes a special wine is trotted out for tasting. None of the guests drive home. All have made arrangements for either a taxi or a limousine shared with friends.

Closed to the general public for that evening, the 56-seat restaurant sells out every event and half the time will have enough wines, and customer demand, to have an overflow dinner the following Tuesday.

A Sophisticated Clientele

Focaccia's patrons are described by Arbesfeld as, "a New York City clientele that lives on Long Island." Most live within 20 miles of the restaurant and regulars account for 75 percent of its business.

"We offer American food prepared with a continental flair," he says, "calling for different wines to maximize the enjoyment of differing food orders. Few individuals want to consume a whole bottle of wine. Our policy is to offer a selection of outstanding half bottles."

Twenty-five different half bottles are offered, with monthly sales of 100 plus.

Many guests choose to finish their meals with a dessert wine. When asked about Port selections, servers or the sommelier bring four bottles to the table and offer a Port tasting — one-ounce portions of each of three different Ports. This is very popular and helps sell a case of Port wine each month, even through the summer.

For guests new to drinking Port wine, LoRusso suggests either a tawny, which is creamy, mellow and slightly sweet, or a white Port, which is easily approachable.

"We use Private Preserve Wine Preserver to keep all of our opened Ports and specialty wines in excellent condition indefinitely," he adds.

34

A Wealth of Fine Wines

As YOU DINE at The Wine Cellar at The Carltun, a sense of awe gradually changes to a feeling of grandeur. Seated amid the trappings of wealth with taste, you view 40,000 bottles of wine behind the glass wall of a vast temperature- and humidity-controlled wine cellar. Offering 1,700 selections, the largest wine list in New York State, The Wine Cellar has been honored with the *Wine Spectator's* Best of Award of Excellence designation.

These are not just any old wines. Interspersed between racks of wine are wooden shipping cases marked with names such as: Petrus 1982, Dominus Napa 1994, Romanée St. Vivant 1995, Lafite Rothschild 1975, Latour 1985, Mouton Rothschild 1982, Beychevelle 1982. You quickly get the point.

"Before the Carltun opened, in late 1995, sommelier Natalia Zalevska and I began amassing the wines for the Wine Cellar, which wouldn't be open until late 1996," says Anthony Capetola, partner in the restaurant with John Tunney. "To get these fine wines from the rarest great vintages we became fixtures at wine auctions run by Sotheby's, Christie's and Morrell, among others. When we opened the Wine Cellar we had 20,000 bottles and offered 700 vintages."

Before each auction, Zalevska would peruse the catalog and determine what wines they wanted and Capetola would keep in constant touch with her by telephone as he bid. In 1995, they spent $154,000 at auctions and $500,000 a year for the next three years.

"The interest in wines keeps growing," says Gil Travalin, sommelier for all of The Carltun's restaurants and executive manager of The Wine Cellar. "While sales of the great classified growths increase every year, there has been a huge demand for wines from the newly developing wine regions worldwide. The coast of Chile, for instance, is a mirror image of California's coast. Because of a lack of government standards, you would be well advised to stick to those wines developed in cooperation with leading French and American winemakers.

"Australia and New Zealand are producing excellent wines that are gaining popularity with our guests. I particularly enjoy introducing guests to one of our 40 red zinfandels from California because it is a fun wine that is ready to drink when released and marries well with foods. It's spicy flavors are new to most people and I frequently hear, 'I didn't know this existed.' These wines are well received by guests asking for a new varietal."

Over 20 premium wines are offered by the glass. Some guests will state: 'I don't like red wine.' This often means that their previous experience with a red wine might have simply been a poor quality wine or a young cabernet sauvignon. If what they are eating would be best enjoyed with an appropriate red wine, servers will offer a taste of what they believe the guests might enjoy. Often the guests will find that they do enjoy a good red wine. Frequently Travalin gives diners in the Palm Court restaurant or Havana (a private cigar club) guided tours of The Wine Cellar — sometimes as many as twenty times a day.

Every Friday night diners can enjoy an eight-course dinner, paired with eight specially selected wines for $95 per person. This dinner is about enjoyment. It is not a wine class. Travalin does visit each table to answer questions that guests may have about the wines or the food.

He always asks about food allergies or dietary restrictions. "On occasion I have structured an eight-course vegetarian dinner with eight appropriate wines to accompany it," he recalls.

While there is only one sitting and a set menu for the special wine dinners, guests have a choice of 8 p.m. or 9 p.m. seating. "This accommodates the wishes of our guests and allows the kitchen time to expertly prepare these made-to-order dinners," he adds.

Napa Valley Lunches by Chef Rodrigo Bernal

Since April 1999, Napa Valley Lunch has been offered in The Wine Cellar. A four-course lunch and a good glass of wine, at $19 per person, has introduced many people to the facility who had heretofore considered it beyond their means.

— A Typical Menu —
Mini bliss potato cup & caviar
Spring tomato and Gorgonzola petite herb salad
Basil oil & balsamic glaze

Choice of:
French roasted chicken over haricots verts with pear chutney and a hint of white balsamic
Thyme pepper-crusted sliced filet mignon over asparagus, roasted onions and potatoes with horseradish aioli
Pan-seared sterling salmon over wild greens in a citrus sauce

Choice of:
Crème Brûlée
Homemade sorbet floating in a melon and strawberry coulis

Plus:
Complimentary glass of wine from our Napa Valley selection

Benefit Tastings

"The First Annual Long Island Food and Wine Classic was held in November 1999 to raise funds for two local charities," says Tunney. "All 20 Long Island wineries participated and 13 fine restaurants, along with our Palm Court restaurant and Wine Cellar, served some of their specialties. At $65 a person, all attendees had an exceptional evening and wanted to know why this couldn't be offered more than once a year. A good question. We will expand the frequency of these events. It was truly 'a symphony of senses.'"

35 London was Never Like This!

EIGHT WINE dinners a year keep things lively at London Lennie's restaurant in Rego Park, New York.

The chef gets a chance to show off his skills and the staff marvels at the heights of creativity and excellence they can produce under his guidance for these special occasions. Guests are delighted by the culinary treat and the opportunity to taste superb wines selected specifically to enhance the food being served.

A maximum of 45 people are seated for a 2-1/2 hour, four-course dinner accompanied by different wines for each course, generally on a Monday night, sometimes on a Tuesday. All sauces are prepared with the wine that accompanies the item being sauced.

A speaker representing the vineyard or the shipper talks about the wines being offered explaining why each wine was matched to the different courses, going from table to table answering individual questions. Sometimes the winemaker will be in attendance.

"Our guests have to be adventuresome because we definitely are," smiles owner Les Barnes. "We frequently serve game dinners. A Thai dinner that matched Alsatian wines with authentically spicy Thai food was particularly challenging for us to find the perfect food and wine pairings."

Themed Dinners

For the first half of 1999, the themed wine dinners were: "Come to California" (March), "Travel to the Outback" (April), "Italy! . . . Italy! . . . Italy!"

(May) and "A Bit of Bubbly & a Lot of Lobster" (June). The Bubbly dinner is so popular that 75 people are accommodated.

"A representative of Moët Champagne builds a Champagne glass pyramid on one of our tables a week before the event," Barnes adds. "On the Champagne evening he brings a saber and dramatically cuts through the bottle at the top of the neck, about six times, smoothly pouring the Champagne into the top glass. Everybody in the restaurant watches Champagne cascade downward until every glass is filled with bubbly and then passed around to the attendees."

Sabering of Champagne was a tradition of the Russian Cossacks that was quickly adopted by the French. The saberer solidly taps the bottleneck twice and then cleanly severs it with a quick upward slash.

Over half of the wine dinner guests are repeat customers, frequently asking, "How are you going to top this one?" It's a challenge that the staff relishes.

"These dinners were begun in 1993 to add excitement for our regular customers," says Barnes. "They give us an opportunity to serve food and wines that are more interesting and unique than people expect to find in a neighborhood restaurant."

As guests found they truly enjoyed the experience of discovery, Barnes had to increase the price for the dinners to allow for the inclusion of more expensive wines. Initially priced at $45 per person, most are now $60, and the Champagne and lobster dinner goes for $85, at this writing. These prices include tax and gratuities.

"General Manager Barry Frommer, myself, the chef and a few others will decide on the themes for a year of wine dinners," says Barnes, "and the chef and his staff will prepare a variety of dishes to fit each theme. We then taste these along with the wines we are considering for each evening. It takes many sessions before we make final decisions on the menu and wine selections."

A $20 deposit is required and there are no substitutions allowed for food or wine. Everything is orchestrated to make for a spectacular experience.

"We found out the hard way that we have to pay close attention to our scheduling of these affairs," says Barry Frommer. "We stay away from July and August, our busiest months, and January and February. We don't schedule an event during national or religious holidays, school closings or vacation times."

A framed sign on an easel greets restaurant patrons with an announcement of each event as it nears and a "Save the Date" postcard is sent to over 2,000 people, promoting the next four events.

Special Selection Wine List

After a wine dinner there are always unopened bottles of wines that are in too short supply to add to the regular wine list and often too pricey to offer by the glass. Periodically, a Special Selection Wine List is presented to guests as follows:

We would like to offer you some very special wines during the month of January (pick your month). These wines have been featured at our wine dinners and now we would like to offer them to you.

Rosemount Estate Cabernet Sauvignon 1994
Coonawarra, Australia. $28.00

Montevina Zinfandel 1995
Amador Count, California. $22.00

Caneros Bighorn Ranch Chardonnay "Reserve" 1996
Napa Valley, California. $35.00

Rosemount Estate Chardonnay "Show Reserve" 1997
Hunter Valley, Australia. $38.00

Michael Picard Pouilly-Fuissé 1996
Chagny, France. $35.00

Thank You for Dining at London Lennie's.
A restaurant doesn't live on wine alone.

For Beer Drinkers

"Many of our guests are beer drinkers," Barnes says. "While most are happy with the American and import standards, a good number want something different. In 1994 we expanded our specialty beer list and, through trial and error, have arrived at a selection of brews that sell consistently well."

The laminated Beer List features a Beer Styles column describing ales and lagers, Pilsners, amber lagers, wheat beers, pale ales, stouts.

Each beer is given a brief comment:

Samuel Smith's Oatmeal Stout – rich, silky and smooth, dry at first, but yielding to a sweet finish. Dense and calming.

Paulaner Pilsner – classic German Pilsner, slightly sweet with an aromatic hop bite and a zesty finish.

Paulaner (Hefe-Weizen) – six percent wheat malt, crisp and dry with a high carbonation and notes of clove. Distinctive and satisfying.

Duvel – thick, rich head, powerful (8.5 percent) and seductive with a complex, deep character. A lingering dryness and perfuminess create a superb finish. (Requires careful pouring).

Pyramid Pale Ale – highly hopped, with an assertive malt character providing a clean dry finish.

Fuller London Pride Ale – medium strength, strong malty base, well developed hops flavors.

Young's Special London Ale – twice named the "Best Bottled Beer in England." A big beer with a powerful hop character on a subtle and quiet malt body.

Affligem Tripel – an intensely intricate beer, spicy notes, strains of chocolate and pear and a smooth coating finish.

Beer of the Month

Draught Beer:

Brooklyn Lager – the pre-Prohibition beer, based on the lager styles that once dominated the New York area, firm malt body, powerful floral aroma, dry and refreshing finish.

Bass Ale (no description needed).

New England Light – all malt, light and refreshing lager style, delicate bouquet.

Seasonal Draught – changing with the seasons.

The 19-seat bar has a raw bar offering clams, oysters, jumbo shrimp cocktail and *fruits de mer* — very popular. Also a great reason for a customer to have another beer or two. Those wanting more substantial fare can order from the menu and eat at the bar. The bar generates a camaraderie that puts single diners at ease and turns newcomers into regulars.

It didn't take long, after the raw bar was added, for somebody to dream up London Lennie's answer to the *Alabama Slammer* — an *Oyster Shooter.* Put a fresh oyster into a tall shot glass and then fill with Champagne. Immediately cover the glass with a coaster (keeping the bubbles). Raise the covered glass and bang it on the bar. Remove the coaster and quickly down the drink. Some nights get pretty noisy at the bar.

Is There Really a London Lennie?

Yes, the menu tells us that at 15, Lennie ran off to sea and spent the next few years in the fishing fleet up to his hips in mackerel. His stint in the merchant marine took him all over the world and he'd head for the local fish market whenever he'd make port. He became an expert at spotting the freshest fish. Within a couple of years of returning to London he owned four fish 'n chips stands.

Lennie (Leonard Barnes) emigrated "to the colonies" in 1959, and opened London Lennie's as a fish 'n chips shop, ably abetted by his wife, Joan. At the time, it was one of seven stores on the street.

The retail fish shop became a restaurant in 1971, and expanded into three adjacent stores that became vacant in 1977, when his son, Les, took over the business. Eleven years later the busy restaurant was able to expand into the remaining three stores.

"Morris Nathanson, known for his exceptional flair in designing seafood restaurants, captured our essence — a neighborhood restaurant with an English touch," says Barnes.

— Welcome to California Wine Dinner —
May 8, 1999

Lobster Thai Stick
with a sweet onion sauce
Hess Collection Chardonnay,
Napa Valley, California 1996

Salad of baby spinach and grilled shrimp
with orange sesame vinaigrette
Gloria Ferrer Pinot Noir,
Sonoma, California 1996

Oven-roasted rack of lamb
with lemon-zested and truffle-whipped potatoes
Sterling Cabernet Sauvignon,
Napa Valley, California 1995

Crème Brûlée
Mirassou Riesling,
Monterey, California 1997

Coffee, Expresso, Cappucino & Tea

$60 per person
Executive Chef, William Demars

36

Winning Combinations

AFTER 15 YEARS of running a sports bar in Tinley Park, Illinois, Carole White and her partner, Vince Didia, had enough of "pick your pasta, pick your soup, Friday night fish fries and Saturday night steaks" with TVs blaring various sports events.

Closing the doors, they embarked on a feverish four months of work. They tore up the floor and tore down the ceiling in order to re-create a warm, comfortable Italian villa. The community was then invited to visit their Farfalla Trattoria and Wine Bar to enjoy fine wines in a non-intimidating atmosphere.

Encouraging Experimentation

"Our policy is to mark wines up double our cost plus 10 percent and offer a glass at one-fourth of the bottle price." says White. "We seat 48 at tables and our new bar seats ten. Guests are encouraged to explore the wines we offer by trying a flight of wines. We present them on a wooden tray with recesses for four wine glasses and a sloped surface on which rests a card displaying the names of the wines selected for tasting." Guests often take the card home with them as a reminder of wines they particularly enjoyed.

The wine list suggests 10 different flights, then adds: "Or create your own flight with any four wines served by the glass."

Some suggested flights are:

Merlot – Italy, Villa Frattina. DOC (single vineyard, Quartarezza) 1997; Cabert, Grave del Friuli 1997; Villa del Re, DOC, Veneto 1997; La Casa di Bacco, DOC, Veneto 1997; $9.50.

Cabernet Sauvignon – La Casa di Bacco, DOC, Italy 1997; Glass Mountain, California 1996; Joliesse, Napa Valley 1995; DeLoach, Cuvée, Sonoma 1994; $11.

Chardonnay — Santa Margarita, Italy 1997; La Casa di Bacco, DOC, Italy 1997; Fog Mountain, California 1997; Heron, Napa Valley-North Coast; $9.50.

Pairing Food and Wine

At first, open only for dinner, the menu offers three, five-course dinners with matching wines, generally priced between $50 to $65. Or diners can order à la carte. Each item on the menu carries an individual price and guests can order the suggested wine for each selection or choose something else from the list. About 80 percent of the guests order à la carte. The menu changes weekly.

A typical five-course dinner with wine pairings offered by Chef Brent Nardi:

Faranita focaccia bread topped with onion and rosemary, $6.
Lagaria Pinot Grigio.

Sugo Di Piselli, Prosciutto Cotto e Panna, conchiglie pasta tossed in a cream sauce of early peas, prosciutto and parmigiano-reggiano, $12.
Chateau Merlot.

Pollo All'Abruzzese Coi Pomodorini e Le Olive, fricasseed chicken with rosemary, white wine, cherry tomatoes and black olives, $16.
Lagaria Chardonnay.

Insalata Di Ceci, chickpea and crisp lettuce salad drizzled with a chickpea vinaigrette, $4.
Bruschetta Di Albiocche, Peschenoci e Susine, apricot, nectarine and plum bruschetta broiled and served with crème fraîche, $6.
Hogue Late Harvest Riesling.

Five courses with wine selections, $59.

Cognacs, liqueurs and dessert wines are also offered after dinner. Popular with those ordering à la carte is the house recommendation: Cognac Pierre Ferrand Ambre Grande Champagne, 10 years old, $6; 20 years old, $15.

Antipasti served at the bar in the summer of 1999 included:

- Broiled goat cheese served with hearty country bread and tomato-basil sauce, $7.50.

- Assorted domestic and imported cheeses accompanied by seasonal fruit, $6 small, $12 large.

- Fresh cantaloupe wedges wrapped in paper-thin slices of prosciutto, $7.50.

- Five gulf shrimp sautéed in olive oil, garlic and fresh herbs, $7.50.

- Bruschetto di Giorno, hearty country bread served chef's choice, $5.

"There is no other restaurant like ours on the South Side of Chicago," says White, "and, after three months' business, it's going well due to strong word-of-mouth."

37 Wine Selection Made Easy

ENTERING THE Harvest Restaurant in Pomfret, Connecticut, the first thing you see is a wall of wine, housed in a see-through, temperature-and humidity-controlled cabinet. A sign informs you that this is only a portion of the restaurant's world class wine collection — a collection that has earned The Harvest the Award of Excellence from *The Wine Spectator* every year since 1988.

It's obvious that they are serious about wine. "While many of our guests are quite knowledgeable about wine," says Sharon Cooper, co-owner with her husband Peter, "we strive to make all of our guests comfortable with the subject."

A Quick Look at Wines

One example: On opening the 17-page wine list you are greeted with The Harvest's Wine Card, a quick-look version of their proprietor's list, providing a user-friendly introduction. It begins with:

> "The 'Little List' will give you recommendations for certain wine and food categories. This is also a section for what we call crossover wines. Let's say you want to move from a white zinfandel to a true white wine that may have similar characteristics — without going too far afield and losing your interest — try a crossover wine."

The crossover wines suggested are: Bonny Doon, Pacific Rim Riesling 1996, Caymus Conundrum 1997 (very popular) and Venezia White Meritage 1995.

On this wine card are also six California chardonnays; five "red wines on the lighter side" from California, France and Spain; and seven robust reds from California and Chile (Los Vascos Cabernet Sauvignon, Domaine Barons de Rothschild).

"While 95 percent of our guests will either order from the larger list or ask a server for a recommendation, the wine card allows all of our guests to relax while deciding which wine they want to enjoy with a meal," Cooper adds.

Also . . .

"For those not caring for an alcohol beverage, but wanting something special, we prominently feature Sutter Home 'Fre' non-alcohol sparkling and white zinfandel. While not big sellers, they are available when desired and our guests appreciate that."

With over 600 wines to choose from, many priced under $15 but a good number ranging from $150 to $250, servers have not tasted most of the wines available. They are encouraged to ask guests for their comments about the wine they have ordered. When another guest inquires about this wine the server can pass on the evaluation.

Wine Dinners

Since the Coopers opened their first Harvest restaurant in 1985, they have offered three or four wine dinners a year, with Chef Peter Cooper crafting unusual pairings of food and outstanding wines. Currently priced at around $55 per person, these events generally attract about 40 people. An open bar is available during the reception hour for those desiring cocktails before their meal. Others can partake of one or more of that evening's wines, along with hors d'oeuvres. A Tax Relief Wine Tasting Dinner held on April 15, 1999 consisted of:

— 6 p.m. to 6:45 p.m —

Reception with hors d'oeuvres, featuring Negociants USA, Inc. and Monsieur Toutant Selections and the wide variety of wines from Australia.

— 7 p.m. onward —

Green Lip Mussels, Japonaise — deep-sea mussels broiled with a ginger miso butter and served on a bed of angel hair pasta with a touch of toasted coconut.

Oxford Landing Sauvignon Blanc 1997.

Shrimp off the Barbe, Cilantro Cream and Risotto Cakes —
coriander-crusted shrimp, crowning a thin risotto cake accented with a zesty cilantro beurre blanc.
Yalumba Chardonnay, Barossa 1997.

Gorgonzola Walnut Crusted Lamb — prime loin of lamb with a toasted walnut and Gorgonzola cheese crust. Sliced and served with roasted garlic Bordelaise sauce.
Oxford Landing Cabernet Sauvignon/Shiraz 1998,
Yalumba Cabernet Sauvignon 1996.

Orange and Watercress Salad
Caramelized Pear Cheese Tarte.
Yalumba Botrytis Semillon 1997, Surprise Wine.

Cigar Events

"Since 1996, we have been offering cigar events twice a year," says Sharon Cooper. "We schedule these for late spring or early fall, when weather permits outdoor smoking and we are not inundated with summer weddings and other parties." These are themed — one offering a selection of single-barrel bourbons and the other a selection of single malt Scotches, along with an assortment of appetizers and cigars.

"These events are for those who want to experience something different on occasion," she adds. "We charge $25 and average a turnout of 30 for each event, mostly male."

Cocktails, Too

People are enjoying cocktails and the martini is king. One page in the wine list offers six martini specials and three specialty drinks, also inviting guests to create a personal favorite. While many enjoy The Harvest's *Chocolate Raspberry Martini* — Absolut Kurant, white crème de cacao and a splash of Chambord served in a martini glass rimmed with shaved chocolate — some will request a special martini that they enjoyed at another restaurant. If they can describe the ingredients, the restaurant's bartenders will expertly re-create the drink for them.

The Black Cat Bistro, with its 20-foot cherry wood bar, is just off the entranceway. Its namesake drink is very popular: *Black Cat* — Bailey's, Frangelico, Marie Brizard Chocolate Royal and white crème de menthe. In the chocolate vein, they sometimes get requests for Black

Russians, substituting Kremlyovskaya chocolate vodka (from Poland) for the regular vodka. Very popular during colder months is the addition of Stolichnaya Vanil to coffee.

"We'll carry brands like Pimms Cup, Peconika - the Hamptons vodka, Parlova Ukraine and others for the few that ask for them," Cooper says. "We are in the hospitality business and want all of our guests to feel special. Having the brands they want, which may be difficult to find elsewhere, reinforces the principle that we care."

Part Seven

Coffee with spirits of all kinds, not just Irish coffee, is going to be the next "hot category" for restaurants and lounges.
— Michael Bonadies

We are determined that each and every customer finds his or her expectations exceeded.
— Drew Nieporent

I had to do something different to grow the business. California wine was my answer. And I decided that I would assemble a wine list to match the quality of the food and allow my guests to order any wine by the glass.
— Mike Amidzich

In effect, I was telling my customers that if they didn't want to consume a full bottle of wine from my award-winning list, they would have to settle for a limited selection of one choice of sauvignon blanc, chardonnay, merlot, cabernet sauvignon, Chianti classico and pinot noir by the glass.
— Dan Marcheano

As I invested the restaurant's profits in building an enormous selection of fine Italian wines, guests kept ordering Chianti and pinot grigio . . . but I kept buying excellent Italian wines from excellent vintages.
— Steve DePietro

Exceeding Customers' Expectations

IT BEGAN with Montrachet restaurant in 1985. Drew Nieporent opened a French restaurant sans pretense in what was then an undesirable neighborhood of New York. "Tribeca? Will anybody show up?" he worried.

Six nights a week, Montrachet offered a $16 prix fixe dinner prepared by Chef David Bouley, who stayed at Montrachet for about a year before striking out on his own. Lunch was also served on Fridays. Shortly after opening, *New York Times* restaurant reviewer Brian Miller gave it three stars. People showed up, even though it taxed their ingenuity to find the restaurant on West Broadway, off White Street — not your convenient East Side Manhattan location.

Bouley's world-class food demanded accompaniment by world-class wines, and Wine Director Daniel Johnnes was up to the task. The restaurant quickly won the *Wine Spectator* Award of Excellence for its wine list and today proudly boasts the Grand Award of Excellence, a rare honor. In 1998, The *Wine Spectator* also declared Montrachet had the "best restaurant wine list in New York City."

Frequently traveling to France to seek out wine discoveries, Johnnes has presented wine dinners every year at Montrachet since its opening. In the fall of 1999 he offered:

1982 First Growths and their Right Bank Equivalents:

The 1982 vintage was the launching pad for the revival of the Bordeaux wine trade after the devastating crash of 1973 . . . the first "vintage of the century" after 1961 . . . these sumptuous wines are beginning to reveal their glory . . . we will taste the best of the best — Château Lafite-Rothschild, Mouton Rothschild, Margaux, Latour, Haut-Brion from the Medoc and Pomerol and St. Emilion estates, Château Petrus, Trotanoy, Cheval Blanc, Ausone and the monumental Le Pin. These stunning wines will be paired with a meal prepared by Montrachet Chef Remi Lauvand. Extremely Limited Seating! $975 per person, all-inclusive.

Le Montrachet "Marquis de la Guiche" with Veronique Drouhin:

Le Montrachet is the vineyard that yields the greatest dry white wine in the world . . . We have a magnificent collection of young and mature wines that will enable you to judge this mythic wine for yourself . . . Prior to dinner, Veronique will lead us through a tasting of recent vintages from Maison Drouhin. Montrachet Chef Remi Lauvand, will prepare a multi-course meal to accompany the Montrachet 1996, 1986, 1976, 1969, 1966, 1964 and 1961 en magnum and other wines. This is a once in a lifetime opportunity! $550 per person, all-inclusive.

This information is mailed quarterly to members of the Burgundy Club who pay yearly dues of $150 for the right of first refusal to attend all wine events Johnnes presents for The Myriad Group, the umbrella that embraces all the restaurants Nieporent has started since Montrachet, or manages.

Virtually all of Montrachet's patrons drink wine with dinner and are quite passionate about wine and its ceremonies. The restaurant earned a nomination for the James Beard Foundation's Best Restaurant in America Award for 1999.

And then they opened. . .

The core group of Drew Nieporent, Martin Shapiro, Michael Bonadies, Daniel Johnnes, Larry Stone and Tracy Nieporent now own or manage 16 restaurants worldwide under the banner of the Myriad Restaurant Group. More are on the way.

Expansion has allowed them to give employees a chance to grow and earn more money while they stay with the organization. "Depth is important," says Tracy Nieporent. "We train two to three people, who can be relied on to back up each key position. When we open a new restaurant we have an experienced cadre ready to transfer to that operation." Drew Nieporent adds, "We're proud that Myriad's restaurants enjoy very low turnover rates. It's a tribute to an operating philosophy that shares profits with employees whose commitment to demanding standards ensures our success."

Tribeca Grill was opened in 1990 in the same Tribeca neighborhood at the urging of Montrachet customer Robert DeNiro, who became a partner in the restaurant. "We created a neighborhood restaurant for the whole world," says Drew Nieporent. "What had once been a Martinson Coffee factory now housed the Tribeca Grill on the ground floor and film industry offices upstairs.

"We were fortunate in obtaining the same bar that had graced two of New York's venerable watering holes — first, Jack Dempsey's on Broadway and later, Maxwell's Plum."

Wine Director David Gordon has brought an innovative approach to the wine list. "I've arranged the list by style and grape varietal, and then by region," he says. "We have an international list with a focus on American wines. For instance, we offer over 50 different zinfandels, the largest list in New York." The groupings on the list are designed to engage restaurant guests in a non-threatening way:

White
Spicy & Aromatic Varietals
Viognier
Sauvignon Blanc
Light, Crisp and Refreshing
American Chardonnay
French Chardonnay
White Half Bottles (9)
Red
American Pinot Noir
French Pinot Noir
Tempranillo
Merlot
American Cabernet Sauvignon
French and Italian Cabernet Sauvignon

Nebbiolo
Sangiovese
Barbera
Zinfandel
Grenache, Syrah, Mourvedre
Syrah, Petite Syrah
Red Half Bottles (14)
Red Magnums (16)

Gordon adds, "We also have several vertical listings of wines that came directly from the wineries to our temperature-controlled cellar." Some of these are:

Pinot Noir
Williams Selyem 'Olivet Lane' Russian River 1996, 1994, 1993.
ZD, Carneros 1995, 1993, 1992, 1991, 1990.
Cabernet Sauvignon: The Harlan Estate, Napa, 1994, 1993, 1992, 1991, 1990, plus ten other estates.

Bordeaux
Château Mouton Rothschild, Pauillac, 1986, 1987, 1982.
Château Latour, Pauillac, 1986, 1975.
Château Lafite Rothschild, Pauillac, 1988, 1982.
Château Cos D'Estournel, St.-Estephe, 1993, 1989, 1988.
Plus additional verticals from Italy, Australia and other regions of France and America.

The last page of the list features 1994 California Cabernet. "Twenty-three wines from this much heralded vintage have been stored in our temperature-controlled cellar since they were purchased," says Gordon. "These wines are beginning to show some of the complexities of age and are ready to be enjoyed."

It's no surprise that the Tribeca Grill received *Wine Spectator*'s Best of Award of Excellence designation in 1998.

The Resurgence of Irish Coffee

It's not just food and wine that draw guests to the restaurant. The bar is very popular. Martini sales are strong, and there are calls for the classic cocktails, single malts and Cognacs. Irish coffee was reintroduced in 1997 and has become a very popular winter drink.

"Coffee with spirits of all kinds, not just Irish coffee, is going to be the next 'hot category' for restaurants and lounges," says Michael Bonadies, director of operations for the Myriad Group. "Vintage Port is also a strong seller and we are seeing calls for Madeira. We continually introduce our guests to new wines and spirits because a high percentage of them are looking for something new."

All staff members are encouraged to sample and learn about new beverages at staff meetings. "First make fans out of the servers and everything else will follow," adds Bonadies.

Tea

Tea is not just for the ladies anymore, at least at Heartbeat restaurant. After hiring James Labe as a host for the new restaurant, management learned that he had managed a teashop in Seattle and was very learned, and enthusiastic, about teas. "With a restaurant that was developed around the concept of heart-healthy food that also tastes great, this was like discovering gold in your backyard," Bonadies says.

Labe became the restaurant's tea sommelier and developed a Tea Menu of eight to twelve varieties that changes seasonally. Strawberry and chrysanthemum herbal teas are also on the list. Fifty to sixty percent of customers order an individually brewed pot of tea, enough for three cups, generally after a meal. On occasion, Labe has paired teas with menu items for regular customers.

Often, business sessions are conducted over tea in the between-meals hours. "Most business people don't care for an alcohol drink during the business day, but find a restaurant meeting more productive than one held at the office," says Bonadies. "Freshly brewed, exotic teas are now a popular part of that meeting."

Fun with the Wine List

Layla, also in New York's Tribeca neighborhood, offers Middle Eastern and Mediterranean cuisine, with some liberties taken. This light-hearted approach is reflected in the wine list.

Seven sparkling wines follow the question: "What do they drink in the French Foreign Legion?" Four rosé wines are listed under: "What to drink with Baba Ghannouj and a Mess of Other Mezze?" Eight white wines are listed after, "What were Cleopatra's favorites?" Another question — "What to drink when lost in the desert?" — produces nine more white wines.

"What wines did Noah bring on the ark?" introduces another nine white wines, rarer and more expensive than the others.

Red wines are listed under these questions: What were King Tut's top reds? — Six wines. What gives the biggest bang for the buck? — Cline Zinfandel 1996, California. What wine is made near the Temple of Bacchus? — Château Musar, Lebanon, 1989, 1988. Which wines are unusual for a Mediterranean wine list but are still delicious? — Nine wines. Which New-World wines have an Old-World taste? — Eleven wines. Which are the wines for romance? — Four wines.

"When given the wine list, people smile, read it thoroughly and frequently try a wine that they have never had before," says Johnnes. "Layla is a fun dining experience for our guests. And this fanciful approach is key to introducing them to wines from Italy, Spain, Morocco, Greece, Guadeloupe and Lebanon that they would never try otherwise."

Cocktails receive the same treatment. Layla specialty cocktails are: *Moroccan Margarita* — Cuervo Gold tequila, pomegranate juice, triple sec and fresh lime juice; *Neapolitan* — Gosling's rum, sour cherry juice and fresh lime juice; *Layla* — Pomegranate juice and sparkling wine; *Cyclone* — Stoli Ohranj, apple schnapps and fresh lemon juice; *Metropol* — Ketel One vodka, rose petal water and dry vermouth; and *Hemingway Daiquiri* — Bacardi rum, grapefruit juice, fresh lime juice and maraschino cherry liquor.

The basic tenet that drives Drew Nieporent and his partners is not anything you haven't heard before. It's the execution of it that separates the successful restaurants from the not so successful. Nieporent sums up their philosophy in one sentence: "We are determined that each and every customer finds his or her expectations exceeded."

SERVER WINE TRAINING SIMPLIFIED

You can now use the same server training program that is used by the Myriad Restaurant Group to cut through the gobbledygook and make wine fun and accessible for you, your staff and your customers.

Sip By Sip, An Insider's Guide to Fine Wine was written by Michael Bonadies, one of the partners in the Myriad Restaurant Group, for those restaurateurs who, for whatever reasons, have been unable to fully train all of their serving staff about wine. Understanding how hectic the business often is, and being all too familiar with the high turnover rate that plagues many restaurants, Bonadies has developed a workbook that functions as the foundation for an ongoing, restaurant-directed wine training program. Or it can be a road map for the self-motivated and curious server. However you use it, you will be ahead of the game. Some of the book's insights:

- Customers want help, guidance and friendly interaction when it comes to wine. They'll let you know if they're not interested. Ask: "Are you in the mood for white wine or red wine? . . . French or California? . . . Young or mature . . . Full or light-bodied? . . . Fruity or very dry?" These questions get the customer involved and help both of you discover what the customer really likes.
- Once a customer's likes have been determined, zero in with three appropriate recommendations in different price categories — low-, medium- and high-priced. Never back a customer into a corner with one single high-priced recommendation that may be a lot more than they want to spend. At the same time, never underestimate a customer's desire, need or willingness to spend money.

If people want to spend money, it's your sacred duty to assist them. And if they don't, then it is up to you to help them find a wine that will represent a great value to them. They'll remember your help and come back.

- It is important to have "safe" wines to recommend, wines which you have found to consistently please your customers. These wines should not be too adventurous or pricey . . . good value and lots of pleasure.
- Bonadies quotes Daniel Johnnes, wine director for Montrachet and other Myriad Restaurant Group restaurants, from his book, *Top 200 Wines:* A white wine served too cold lacks flavor ... a red wine served too warm loses freshness and balance. The right temperature for wine for fullest enjoyment is:
  - Champagne and Sparkling . . . very cold — 40 degrees F.
  - Sauternes and Sweet Wines . . . very cold — 40 degrees F.
  - Light Whites . . . well chilled — 45 degrees F.
  - Medium/Full Whites . . . Very cool — 48-50 degrees F.
  - Rich and Great Whites . . . Cool — 52-55 degrees F.
  - Light Reds . . . Slightly chilled — 55 degrees F.
  - Medium Reds . . . Cool — 60 degrees F.
  - Full Reds . . . Room temperature — 65 degrees F.

Topics covered run the gamut from how to taste, sell and serve wine to what to do when a wine is returned and hundreds of other points.

Copies of this workbook are available for $20 from Jordan Winery, (who, along with Joseph Phelps Vineyards, partnered in producing this book), call (707) 431-5250.

39 The Place for Italian Wines

STEVE DEPIETRO, owner of Il Cigno restaurant in Scarsdale, New York, determined in 1991, that any increase in profits from beverage alcohol sales would have to come from his wine list. Guests were ordering one cocktail before dinner, at most, and were not lingering over an after-dinner drink.

Since Il Cigno was well known and respected for its Italian cuisine, he began to buy Italian wines available from the best producers — especially Piedmont wines from the great vintages of 1989, 1990 and a very good 1988.

"As I invested the restaurant's profits in building an enormous selection of fine Italian wines," DePietro recalls, "guests kept ordering Chianti and pinot grigio."

It wasn't until John Mariani wrote a rave review of the restaurant in a local paper in January 1993, that a new clientele was attracted — one that appreciated the opportunity to enjoy Italy's finest wines at very reasonable prices. By 1994, there were 400 Italian wines on the list and special winemaker dinners attracted 40 to 50 or more guests, six times a year.

Building a Wine Reputation

"Our wine distributor salesmen let us know when winemakers from Italy are visiting this area, and we can often arrange for them to take part in a special dinner event matching our Northern Italy-inspired foods with their wines," DePietro says. "We constantly add to our mailing list by requesting business cards from our regular customers who order a bottle of wine with dinner."

Sometimes distributor salesmen get so enthused about an event that they reserve tables for themselves and guests.

These dinners created excitement and made a statement that Il Cigno was a destination for Italian wines. Business grew by 35 percent a year during 1993 and 1994, leveling off for the next two years and then spurting ahead again in 1997, when Il Cigno finally gained widespread recognition for the magnificence of its fine Italian wine offerings.

. . . and a Wine List

"Even when guests were ignoring these wines in the early years, I kept buying excellent Italian wines from excellent vintages," DePietro stresses. "Now, in 1999, we have over 750 bottles on our list, many very rare wines only available here. While we price the prestige wines at market prices, there are incredible values for the wine knowledgeable. The Piedmont vintages of 1995, 1996 and 1997 are comparable to the great vintages of 1988, 1989 and 1990. I am currently loading up on '95s and '96s, and will be buying '97s when they come on the market."

By 1998, the restaurant was so well established as the place to go for Italian wines that winemaker dinners were reduced to two a year. Held during winter months, this heightened their special appeal for the core group of super wine drinkers who regularly spend $50 or more for a bottle of wine.

The Return of Cocktails

As cocktails made a comeback, esoteric brands of high quality vodka and single malt Scotch were featured prominently on the back bar alongside the super premiums that are in strong demand.

"We like to introduce our guests to brands of spirits that they may not have heard about or that they may know about but have not yet tried," says DePietro. "A visit to our restaurant, for food or drink, should be a visit of discovery."

The Making of a Chef

Steve DePietro was a breakfast cook in a hospital in 1974 and soon decided that he didn't like working in a restaurant kitchen. Returning to college, he earned a degree in 1980 and had a decision to make: Invest $20,000 to earn a graduate degree or go back to work as a cook and make $500 a week.

He opted to give the restaurant business another try and worked in Manhattan restaurants for the next four years, the last two and a half as a chef. The food revolution was happening and, wanting to give full expression to his own style, he returned to his family's restaurant — Il Cigno in Scarsdale, New York.

His goal was to take this popular Italian restaurant up another notch. "I believe in working within strict parameters. Instead of a broad Continental-style menu, I focused on the foods of northern Italy," he states, "authentic, regional cuisine in a reworking of classical dishes as I interpret them for my guests.

"I visit the Hunt's Point market religiously and handpick the vegetables, meat and fish that will be served to our guests," he adds. "And I do my own butchering. I get the quality that I want while saving a considerable amount of money."

His advice to aspiring restaurateurs is simply to know what you are and where you want to go.

40

Half Bottles to the Rescue

"ADVERSITY SEEMS to bring out the best in me," says Dan Marcheano, owner of The Arches Restaurant in Newport Beach, California. "When California decreed that nobody could smoke in restaurants anymore, we lost a lot of our regulars. Other restaurants added or expanded outdoor patio dining where their customers could enjoy a smoke if they wished, but we don't have room to do that.

"In the seventeen years that I have owned this restaurant, I have prided myself on attracting and retaining a highly professional staff and serving only the finest quality of fresh food, often prepared tableside. We've won *Wine Spectator*'s top wine award every year since 1983 and *Zagat* says, 'The best Steak Diane anywhere.' Now I had to take this fine restaurant up another notch."

Expanding Wine Sales

Marcheano analyzed his wine sales, and noted that by-the-glass represented 25 percent of the total. "In effect, I was telling my customers that if they didn't want to consume a full bottle of wine from my award-winning list, they would have to settle for a limited selection of one choice of sauvignon blanc, chardonnay, merlot, cabernet sauvignon, Chianti Classico and pinot noir . . . by the glass," Marcheano remembers.

This was a no-brainer. He immediately queried his wine suppliers about the availability of a consistent supply of quality half bottles. Now Marcheano has over a dozen choices in half bottles, including four chardonnays, five cabernet sauvignons and an Opus One. Overall wine sales have climbed and, while by-the-glass still accounts for 25 percent (of a larger base), half bottles account for 12 percent, while not cutting into full-bottle volume.

Reintroducing the Pleasures of Port

"As Cognac sales declined along with the exodus of cigar smokers, I decided to reintroduce my clientele to the deliciousness of Port wine," Marcheano says. "When a group was celebrating a special event and had finished their meal, I would approach their table with a bottle of Port and some glasses, offering them a complimentary tasting. For any children in the group the staff would prepare a banana flambé."

A typical response was: "Thank you, I haven't even thought about Port in ten years or more." Some then ordered a second glass; others ordered Port on subsequent visits. Sales of Port wine have soared to 15 bottles a week.

The Continuing Challenge

"We haven't recouped all of the business we have lost because of the smoking ban, but this restaurant has thrived and grown since 1922 and we're going to continue that tradition," Marcheano says with a smile.

Celebrities have sung the praises of The Arches Restaurant since Hollywood discovered Orange County. The accolade Marcheano treasures most is a letter reprinted on his menu:

October 29, 1998

Dear Dan:

Congratulations on receiving Wine Spectator's Award of Excellence for the 15th straight year.

Margrit and I commend you for everything that you do at The Arches to enhance one of life's greatest pleasures — fine wine and cuisine shared with good friends while surrounded by art and music. When I was there to see you, I'll never forget how much you made me feel like family.

Sincerely,
Robert Mondavi

4 Pizza and . . . Wine?

"MAN DOES Not Live By Pizza Alone."

She/he also lives by:
290 Wines by the Glass
Escargot
Black Seafood Lasagna
B.B.Q. Ribs
Wild Boar Ravioli
Crab Cheese Spinach Melt
Tortellini Supreme
Pasta a la Pescatora
Pasta Florentine
Chicken Marsala

Pizza Man
1800 East North Avenue
Milwaukee, WI 53202
(414) 272-1745
Conveniently located 2,162 miles due east of Napa in Milwaukee, Wisconsin.

You have just read page one of Pizza Man's wine list booklet. The cover announces: "Award of Excellence" — Ten-time Award Winner, *The Wine Spectator.*

The next 15 pages list 290 wines available by the glass or bottle. The more expensive wines are asterisked, indicating a minimum order of two glasses from marked bottles.

"This guarantees that I won't take a loss on a bottle if somehow it slips through the cracks and turns bad before it has been completely sold," says owner Mike Amidzich. "I use Private Preserve wine preserver to put a three-layer shield of inert gases between the remaining wine in the bottle and oxygen, so it's rare for a wine to turn. But the asterisk also alerts the guest that this is a fine wine he or she is drinking."

Thirty years ago, Pizza Man opened as a small pizza place that delivered locally. Over time the menu grew to include creative Italian dishes and more space allowed for a 55- to 60-seat dining room. After 20 years, most of the business was pizza and beer, some spirits.

Growing a Business with California Wines

"I had to do something different to grow the business," Amidzich remembers. "California wine was my answer. And I decided that I would assemble a wine list to match the quality of the food and allow my guests to order any wine by the glass."

The immediate response was not deafening. Slowly word spread and new faces began showing up — and coming back with friends. Twice-a-month wine dinners were very successful. Too successful, Amidzich decided, since these dinners encouraged lingering, cutting into the customer turnover that produced 350 to 400 dinner customers every day.

After a couple of years he reduced the frequency to once a month and four years later he stopped them. "It was too much work," Amidzich says, "and they had accomplished what I wanted. Most people were ordering wine along with our cuisine features. Open 365 days a year from 4 p.m. to 2 a.m., we are now consistently turning tables seven times a night."

This has been accomplished with very little advertising and virtually no support from the local press. The growth has been internally generated, fueled by very positive word-of-mouth. The restaurant atmosphere is relaxed and casual, servers are young, many of them part-timers from local colleges.

Other than the boss, there is no sommelier. Guests peruse the wine list and make their own selections. Most of the clientele has become wine knowledgeable, sometimes just through trial and error.

If you are Internet-savvy, key in www.Wineman.com. You will be amazed. Not only has Amidzich creatively put his wine list on a Pizza Man home page, he has listed over 2,400 wine-award-winning restaurants in the United States. Your restaurant might be listed if you have won a prestigious award for your wine list. Take a look, most restaurateurs on the list don't know anything about it.

"This is not a money-making endeavor on my part," he says. "I don't charge for the listings nor do I charge those restaurants listed in red, that link to their home pages. Some listed restaurants have an extensive presence on this site. It's just something I want to do."

42 Wine Tastings Generate Dinner Business

TWO HUNDRED year-round residents of Naples, Florida, and fifty seasonal refugees from the cold, gladly pay Cuisine Management $25 per year for membership in its Cellar Club.

This entitles them to 25 percent discounts on wine tastings, ten percent discounts on wine dinners, first priority on reservations for these events and two annual complimentary wine tastings.

There's also a ten percent discount on case wine purchases at Tony's Off Third, a unique combination of neighborhood bakery, fine wine shop and outdoor cafe offering freshly prepared salads and sandwiches as well as desserts, bread, pastries and a variety of premium coffees.

"Where wine accounted for 40 percent of our restaurant's beverage revenue in 1992, by 1999 it represented 60 percent," says Wine Director Sukie Honeycutt. "As our customers' wine sophistication grows, they look to us to introduce them to new wines from all parts of the world."

The monthly wine tastings at Terra restaurant attract 60 to 75 guests to sample eight to twelve wines and are generally offered on weeknights between 5 p.m. and 6:30 p.m. for a $15 general admission. More than half of the attendees remain for dinner at the Mediterranean-style grill offering casual, affordable cuisine, often purchasing a glass or a half bottle of a wine that impressed them earlier.

"In addition to over 16 different wines available by the glass," adds Honeycutt, "we offer at least ten wines by the half bottle. This allows more freedom in matching wines with different courses to meet different tastes."

Several times a year themed, sit-down wine tastings are held in the restaurant. From 5 p.m. to 6 p.m., six to eight wines from a particular region or winery will be tasted and discussed.

This interest in fine wine is reflected in Tony's Off Third Wine Catalog which offers:

Mixed Samplers — Sukie's Private Stash — $400.
A six-pack of incredibly scarce California reds: Silver Oak Alexander Valley Cabernet Sauvignon '95, Shafer Hillside Select Cabernet Sauvignon '95, Dominus '96, Joseph Phelps Insignia '95, Paradigm Cabernet Sauvignon '95, Dalla Valle Cabernet Sauvignon '96.

Grab Bags — $275 Package
A case of premier cabernets, merlots, pinot noirs, chardonnays and sauvignon blancs, with wines valued as high as $35 a bottle.

Tony's Off Third takes coffee very seriously. A pamphlet, *If you don't know BEANS . . .*, tells guests that it has captured the art of brewing the perfect cup and explains how it is done at Tony's Off Third. For those purchasing coffee beans to brew at home or office, these tips are given:

- Buy only fresh whole beans and grind only what you will brew that day.
- Store your coffee beans in your freezer to retard loss of flavor and aroma.
- Always brew with filtered cold water.
- Never boil coffee — use a drip or filter system.
- Discard grounds immediately after brewing. Condensation from the grounds will make brewed coffee bitter or smoky over time.
- When kept warm coffee will only remain at peak freshness for 15 minutes. After that it's downhill.
- Clean your coffee grinder and brewing equipment after each use. Trace oils will mar your next brewed pot.

Who said life, or the restaurant business, is easy?

43 Wine Flights of Fancy

CORK'S STEAK HOUSE, a wine and cocktail bar in Naples, Florida, originally opened as a wine bar with a limited food menu in January 1998. "Open a place here in January or February and you'll be successful for four months," says owner Cloyde Pate. "Then comes the summer crunch when you better have a good local following, or it's goodbye."

Listen to Your Customers

Pate listened to local customers perched at a bar that, in 1933, had been the focal point of the Alibi Club in Chicago. Like those long-ago drinkers, his patrons wanted more of a choice than wine, no matter how good the selection was.

That June, a full line of spirits was added and locals found it the ideal place to visit after having dinner at nearby restaurants. Being open until 1 a.m. also attracted many of the employees of those restaurants who enjoyed unwinding with a fine Cognac, a glass of Port or a glass of wine.

"We're cigar friendly," says Beverage Manager Dan Romelo, "and our selection of fine Ports by the glass accounts for sales of about six bottles a week."

Featured Flights

From the beginning people enjoyed having a choice of 48 wines by the glass and the opportunity of trying new wines in flights of three. A flight of three chardonnays, offered two-ounce servings of Kendall Jackson Camelot, La Crema Sonoma and Castillo Banfi Italy for $9.75.

A flight of red zinfandels was also offered for $9.75 with two-ounce servings of Ravenswood,

Alexander Valley Sin Zin and Rodney Strong OV. Other flights offered included cabernets and sauvignon blancs. Deloach White Zinfandel, Columbia J. Riesling and J. Droughin Pouilly-Fuissé was an unusual selection that attracted a number of requests from ladies.

A featured flight offered two-ounce tastes of Swanson Vineyards' Cabernet Sauvignon, Merlot and Sangiovese for $10.95 or allowed a guest to choose a six-ounce glass of any Swanson varietal for $10.25.

Flights are changed every few months as good buying opportunities allow for exceptional values for Cork's clientele. Weekly, three reds and three whites are featured as end-of-bin specials.

Table servers utilize a wine carrier holding three glasses for bringing wine flights to the tables and a four-glass carrier for regular wine service. "Since introducing these carriers we've reduced glass breakage by 40 percent," says Pate.

Commenting on where consumer tastes are heading, he says red zinfandels, merlots and meritage wines are coming on strong.

Part Eight

Not every member of a social or business group wants an alcohol drink. And some drinkers would appreciate an alternative as the evening progresses. Creativity is the imperative to make this work and we, in the hospitality business, are the most creative people I know.

— Joe Fassler

If you are still thinking that you're in the alcohol business, you're leaving money on the table. You are in the entertainment business, and exceeding your guests' expectations at every turn is a straight road to success.

— Robert Plotkin

A significant number of people are bored with diet colas and are willing to pay a premium price for an interesting diet drink. While accounting for 15 percent of soda sales, these drinks bring in almost half of our dollar volume for soda sales.

— Ira Freehof

It's Time For Creative Non-Alcohol Drinks

44

by Joe Fassler

AS A hospitality operator since 1963, and the immediate past chairman of the National Restaurant Association (May 1998 to May 1999), I've learned to listen, observe and recognize what our customers are really saying. This wonderful experience has taught me to learn the "whys" of their actions.

To win over today's new beverage customers, operators must learn from others who had to win over their new customers.

When you review the success of specialty coffee companies, specialty bagel shops with flavored bagels, the variety of pretzel companies with flavored toppings and the many different types of doughnut, muffin and bun shops, all of which have added billions of dollars in sales to our $354 billion industry, you will recognize a new opportunity for beverage sales.

New signature non-alcohol drinks will create excitement and the coming of age of a new beverage category. Done right, this will be effective for the casual restaurant, the formal hotel dining room, lounges and pubs.

Not every member of a social or business group wants an alcohol drink. Some drinkers would appreciate an alternative as the evening progresses. Creativity is the imperative to make this work and we, in the hospitality business, are the most creative people I know.

— Joe Fassler is president and ceo of ProDine, Inc., formerly known as Restaura.

45

Don't Leave Money on the Table

by Robert Plotkin

IF YOU are still thinking that you're in the alcohol business, you are leaving money on the table. You are in the entertainment business, and exceeding your guests' expectations at every turn is a straight road to success.

Non-alcohol beverages (NAB) are now an important part of the restaurant industry's profit structure. I see you nodding your head as you note how many Diet Cokes you sold last night . . . virtually 100 percent profit.

What about people who prefer non-caffeine diet sodas? Do you offer Diet Sprite or Diet 7-Up? If you don't, your customers won't say anything but next time they might opt for a restaurant that gives them that choice. Meantime, you've lost a profit opportunity. Fast food restaurants have latched on to the importance of non-caffeine diet sodas . . . for a very good reason.

Who else says so? The Cowboy Palace Saloon in Chatsworth, California, for one. Billing itself as "the last real honky tonk," with live Country Western music and a 15-horse hitching post, it attracts a clientele of working cowboys and cowgirls as well as "part-time cowboys." You might expect a hard-drinking group of customers.

Guess again. Partners Bob Rustigian and Rhonda Sarnicola created some alcohol-free specialty drinks, added non-alcohol beers, Snapple beverages and Raymond Old Style sodas and presented them on a special menu, expecting a mild response.

"Sales took off in a big way, almost immediately," Rustigian told me. "We sell a fair amount of alcohol but there are times when people want to have a drink that isn't a drink."

Develop a Marketing Strategy

Whatever your customers are drinking now, give them a non-alcohol drink alternative to switch to when they feel they have had enough alcohol and are concerned about driving home. Create and present these drinks with the same flair and production values as your regular cocktails and price them comparably.

The same non-alcohol flavorings that Starbucks and other coffee purveyors flavor their offerings with can be used to make cocktails as traditional as a grasshopper (Remember that? A one-time big favorite with the ladies.) or a daiquiri. Suppliers have ample recipes or ask your bartenders to experiment and see what they can come up with.

For beer drinkers offer at least two or more N/A beers. Many will appreciate being able to unobtrusively shift gears.

Even wine drinkers now have N/A wines available to them, as well as some tasty sparkling N/A wines (sometimes euphemistically called Champagne). At a table celebrating with real Champagne, offer this alternative to any non-drinkers and give it the full treatment, wine stand or bucket, Champagne flute, cork popping. You'll make a friend.

For the Health Conscious

Energy drinks have long been popular in Europe and are fast catching on with the young and the thirty-somethings. California and Florida saw the first surge, but now these drinks are everywhere. These products are specially formulated to deliver biologically active ingredients — such as herbal extracts, vitamins, minerals and pharmaceutical-grade amino acids — in great-tasting beverages.

These are not the same as sport drinks or isotonic beverages that merely replenish body fluids. Their makers say that these products stimulate the metabolism and rejuvenate by replenishing the mind and body with energy.

The leading brands contain caffeine as a catalyst for the absorption of the B vitamins. Most also contain the guarana berry from South America (a subtle stimulant), ginseng, amino acids and vitamins.

If you draw an active late-night crowd, many will ask for an energy drink for rejuvenation. Bartenders also have created numerous energy drink cocktails that get significant calls.

The same crowd generally also enjoys smoothies and slushes, with and without rum, tequila, and so forth. Adult sodas are a new fad. I know it sounds like an oxymoron, but Californians are clamoring for Skeleteens, a line with names like Brain Wash, Love Potion #69 and Black Lemonade — herbal-based sodas with a singular spicy flavor that boggles the imagination.

Regular lemonade is fast becoming a must at nightclubs and trendy bars . . . with or without the Jack Daniels.

We all know what's happening with coffee and bottled water. When the people who keep chic coffee shops in the black dine at your place, dazzle them with your coffee pyrotechnics . . . both with and without spirits.

After all, you are in show biz!

Robert Plotkin is the chief contributing editor of the American Mixologist Newsletter *and author of numerous books on bartending and beverage management, including* Increasing Bar Sales: Creative Twists to Bigger Profits. *He can be reached at Barmedia, (800) 421-7179 or e-mail: barinfo@barmedia.com.*

Non-alcohol specialty drinks should be as delicious and sophisticated as those that contain alcohol. Since people taste with their eyes before lifting up a drink, select the glassware and garnish for each drink carefully. Give each drink its own special flair. Here are a few examples of dynamic alcohol-free specialties:

Frozen Strawberry Tea
4 oz. English
breakfast tea (brewed)
1 oz. sweet-and-sour
2 tbsp. sugar
1/2 cup frozen strawberries
Blend with ice

Blueberry Lemon Fizz
6 oz. blueberry yogurt
1 cup lemon sherbert
2 oz. lemon-lime soda
3 dashes grenadine
Blend with ice

Raspberry Kiss
6 oz. Ocean Spray Cran-Raspberry Drink
1 oz. orange juice
1/2 oz. Rose's lime juice
Shake and strain
Fill with club soda

Coco Mocha
4 oz. coconut cream syrup
2 oz. cold black coffee
1/2 tsp. chocolate syrup
Blend with ice
Pour into a coffee mug
Garnish with whipped cream
Sprinkle nutmeg on top

No-Load Margarita
1 oz. non-alcohol triple sec
1 oz. orange juice
1-1/2 oz. sweet 'n sour
1/2 oz. Rose's lime juice
Blend with ice
Splash of club soda (optional)
Lime wheel garnish

46 Go With the Coffee Flow

By 1996 it was clear to Nick Castronova that he was fighting an uphill battle trying to stem the slide in sales of after-dinner drinks in his fine dining restaurant, The Lamplighter, in Rochester, New York.

"After a cocktail before dinner and wine with the meal," he remembers, "my guests would say they had to drive home, order a coffee and some refills, pay the check and leave. They were concerned about even approaching the level that would be considered driving-while-impaired."

He decided to go with the flow and give his customers what they wanted, in a way that would encourage them to linger, and at the same time rebuild his check averages.

Special Coffee and Dessert Pairings

"We have glamorized our presentation of espresso, cappuccino and flavored coffees, suggesting dessert pairings from among biscotti, tiramisu, lemon ice and rich chocolate selections," Castronova says. "Our guests have been very receptive to this and about one half of those ordering a special coffee will also order dessert." Helping build dessert sales is the policy of serving an over-large portion that couples are encouraged to share. Frequently heard at tables is, "I'll order dessert if you'll help me."

Specialty coffees are also offered with a variety of spirits and are popular with guests not concerned with driving.

Promotions Center on Food and Festivity

On Monday and Friday nights the restaurant offers steamed clams for $4 a dozen. "We're selling at our cost and people pack our lounge on those nights," he adds. "This is a promotion that benefits our regulars and encourages them to visit us a second or third time during the week.

"At holiday times we look like a page out of a catalog. A starburst of multi-colored lights and seasonal decorations enliven the dull days of winter and welcome the onset of spring. It gives people a reason to plow through the snow that upstate New Yorkers are all too familiar with."

Newsletters and birthday cards alert over a thousand nearby residents to what is happening now and what to look forward to. "We try to give our guests what they want and pleasantly surprise them at the same time," smiles Castronova.

47 New York's Coolest Pleasures

EGG CREAMS to die for are made at the table in Ira Freehof's two Comfort Diners in New York City. A 12-ounce milkshake glass is filled one-third with milk and then given a good squirt of seltzer water. Chocolate, strawberry or vanilla syrup is added, to taste. After stirring, the seltzer bottle and syrup are left on the table for customers to fine-tune the egg cream to their taste. All this for $2.50.

People come back.

"I opened the original Comfort Diner in Manhattan on East 45th Street in February 1996, because I believed it was time to bring the old-fashioned diner, with good food at very reasonable prices, back to Manhattan's East Side," remembers Freehof. "A year later, I opened a second diner at 86th Street and Lexington Avenue. People appreciated something different."

Part of the 'something different' was the egg creams. Another part was the return of milkshakes to the big city . . . in a big way. Large signs in each diner proclaim, "The City's Best Milkshake" and one month a year is designated "The Month of Milkshakes." An August calendar promotes a different flavor for each day and window signs announce: "We're now into Day 12 (changing each day, of course) of our August Milkshake Festival. Today's special is Banana Split." Among the other flavors are: Blueberry Cheesecake, Raspberry Swirl, Not Hot Hot Chocolate, Piña Colada and S'mores.

The list of sodas is extensive and definitely not

boring. No-sugar Birch and Diet Orange Cream are just two of the many diet sodas offered. "A significant number of people are bored with diet colas and are willing to pay a premium price for an interesting diet drink," adds Freehof. "While accounting for 15 percent of soda sales, these drinks bring in almost half of our dollar volume from sodas."

Decaf Iced Tea

Opening day of the first Comfort Diner was as frenetic as is usually the case. "After four glasses of iced tea, I was buzzing," Freehof says. "Serving free refills on iced tea to customers, I became concerned on their behalf and quickly switched to decaf iced tea. We don't call special attention to it unless a customer requests decaf iced tea. Then we tell him that is what we serve. Everybody is happy and leaves without an added caffeine buzz."

In the year 2000, he expects to have a liquor license. "Weekend brunches in New York are big on Bloody Marys and Champagne, which we cannot offer now," Freehof says. "I don't expect to do a cocktail business but I do expect we'll attract many more people to our brunches."

This gives you some idea of why *Gourmet* magazine called his restaurant: "The Best Diner in New York."

Part Nine

Dave Steadman's

Restaurant Scene

Editor's Note

Dave Steadman's Restaurant Scene

The Visits You Can't Make

A new concept in newsletters, *Dave Steadman's Restaurant Scene,* will debut on April 18, 2000. With the expertise garnered from years of covering the food, beverage and hospitality industry as a journalist, Dave Steadman will make the competitive visits you don't have time to make yourself.

Every two weeks (except for July, August and December) you'll receive a four-page report similar to what you see in the preview issue on the following pages. Twenty times a year you'll get Dave's easy-to-read, to-the-point report filled with ideas you can use to improve your restaurant's bottom line.

You can subscribe anytime during 2000 at the charter rate of $75 for a one-year subscription, $130 for a two-year subscription. Please send your check or money order, in U. S. funds, to: Spirited Living, 38 Broadway, Greenlawn, NY 11740. For foreign orders please add $30 U. S. for each year.

Dave Steadman's

Restaurant Scene

THE VISITS YOU CAN'T MAKE

PREMIER ISSUE • 2000

The Cooper Experience

Strolling along 58th Street between Fifth and Sixth Avenues in Manhattan, you see people in front of you stopping and staring. You stop and stare also. Looking into an attractive cocktail lounge, your eyes are fixed on a drop-dead beautiful 1966 Austin Healy sitting there waiting for you to drive it away.

And the menu tells you that if you are willing to part with $40,000, you can do just that. Or you can savor a *Courvoisier VS Stinger* for only $12 while you enjoy a Punch Gran Cru Monarcas cigar at a table across from the car.

Two weeks later there will be a different classic car in that space. The menu at Cooper's Classic Cars & Cigar Bar also lists a 1952 Aston Martin Logonda Cabriolet (previously owned by Jack Nicholson) for $85,000. The suggested drink for viewing this car is an *Absolut Citron Cosmopolitan* and the cigar is Royal Jamaica, Churchill. Easier on the wallet is the 1976 Cadillac El Dorado Convertible for $20,000. For watching this car, the menu suggests the *Cooper Classic* — Beefeater gin, grapefruit juice, Campari and a splash of Cointreau. The cigar is Cooper's own blended cigar, Corona. Of course, there are many more classic cars, cigars and cocktails.

After a bit, as you listen to the music of Sinatra, Billie Holliday, Peggy Lee and others, you'll walk around the room to take a closer look at the large black and white photos of famous Hollywood kissing scenes mounted on light boxes. Burt Lancaster and Deborah Kerr in the surf, *From Here to Eternity*. Ali McGraw and Ryan O'Neal, *Love Story*. Audrey Hepburn and George Peppard, *Breakfast at Tiffany's.* Among many others is a picture of Elliot Cuker and his wife sitting in a Bentley. While Cuker has appeared on the Broadway stage and on TV, his appearance on the walls of Cooper's has more to do with the fact that he and his wife

continued . . .

The Cooper Experience

own the lounge as well as a sister company, Cooper Classic Cars, housed in an old church in Greenwich Village for over 20 years.

"I opened Cooper's Classic Cars and Cigar Bar in 1997 to reflect what I would like to visit, a place with a feeling of romance," says Elliot Cuker. "Having been an actor and a lover of classic cars and classic cigars, I determined to combine all of my loves and, at the same time, expand my personal experiences."

Realizing that guests would sometimes want food with their drinks, he made arrangements with a nearby restaurant to fulfill and deliver orders that his staff called in. Cooper's customers have an extensive, high quality menu to choose from without necessitating Cuker's investment in kitchen and staff.

Guests are invited to regard Cooper's as an Art Emporium. All of the cars, art and custom furniture may be purchased along with magnificent humidors and pre-Castro Cuban cigars.

Two-and-a-Half Cases of Galliano Every Saturday Night

How often have your bartenders dusted off the Galliano bottle sitting forlornly on your back bar? At Poor Red's in El Dorado, California, the bartenders are too busy pouring Galliano for any dust to collect. Would you believe two-and-a-half cases of Galliano poured every Saturday night? In a town with a population of 160.

The largest seller of Galliano in the world, this restaurant sells three percent of all Galliano sold in America. Originally a stage stop on the Wells Fargo route, post-World War II travelers to California's gold country spread the word about its great barbecued ribs. Fifty-two tons of ribs are sold in one year. Some Sundays, the dining room's 34 seats will accommodate over 400 people.

Today three worldwide travel guides extol its virtues to Europeans heading for the USA. Only now it's not just ribs that are recommended, but also its specialty drink, the *Golden Cadillac,* invented by Poor Red's bartender Frank Klein in the early 1950s.

A couple walked into the bar and the husband, bursting with pride at finally owning a brand new Cadillac, asked Frank to create a drink to commemorate the occasion. Turning to the back bar, the first thing Frank saw was the towering Galliano bottle. He poured an ounce and a half into a mixer, added an ounce and a half of white crème de cacao and about three ounces of half-and-half cream. Blending it with ice, he strained it into a Champagne glass, which he thought fitting for this celebration. (This was when Champagne was served in three-ounce saucer glasses.) The remainder of the drink was poured into a five-ounce water glass and placed alongside the Champagne glass. He then asked what was the color of the car? You know the answer — gold. And so was born the Golden Cadillac drink. Other customers at the bar demanded a taste of this new concoction and they liked it.

On an average Saturday night 240 people will eat at the restaurant and also consume over 400 Golden Cadillacs. Over 40 years after its creation, people still like the drink.

"And demand is not slackening," says Mike Speegle, one of the five bartenders. "I've been bartending here since 1982, and we serve the drink just as Frank did for that first Golden Cadillac customer. When Dave Chapdelaine took over the restaurant about 1993, he said 'don't change anything; if it ain't broke don't fix it,' and people keep coming back."

Known as a fun place, on any given night you might see stretch limos, a Rolls Royce or two, Ford pick-ups and a couple of Harleys parked outside, their drivers laughing together and sipping Golden Cadillacs at the bar.

All staff members wear Poor Red's shirts sporting the Galliano logo and the Golden Cadillac drink. These and other souvenirs are for sale to customers with net proceeds going into an employees' retirement fund. Over $20,000 is raised annually for the fund.

It's too bad your customers don't like Golden Cadillacs.

A Different Happy Birthday Greeting

If your restaurant is in Pennsylvania, Nissley Vineyards can help you make your guests' special occasions very special with labels designed to be personalized to commemorate any event celebration in quantities as small as one bottle or as many as you would like.
Their table wines are very good, as are their fruit wines, and prices are reasonable.
For specific information ask for Judy Nissley at (717) 426-3514 or (800) 522-2387 in Pennsylvania. Nissley Vineyards & Winery Estate is located in Bainbridge.

Just Having Fun

Never a cover charge. No velvet ropes. Everybody gets a high-energy greeting: "Hi! We're glad you're here." For those interested in lunch or dinner: "A waitress will be right with you."

Most customers head for one of the five bars to play pool or watch one of 101 TV sets with satellite hook-ups that bring in every sports event that's being aired — football, basketball or title fights. No charge to see a Tyson fight.

Over 500 people will pack both floors of Dublin's, on Sunset Boulevard in West Hollywood, California, most nights of the week. The early evening crowd ranges from 25 to 35 years old and the late-nighters range from 21 to 30 years old.

"We offer 56 beers, 15 on tap at our first floor bars," says Bartender Jim Pastorio. "Upstairs we only offer bottled beers. Each of our 18 bartenders has a special drink that he or she is known for. Right now our hottest drink is the *Apple Martini* — Absolut, Apple Pucker, sweet-and-sour and a splash of 7-Up or Sprite. It's flying."

Evening customers at the downstairs bars listen to alternative rock music, while upstairs the room pulses to a Top 40 beat.

"We have something going every night," says owner Kat Johnson. "Every Monday is Models Night, which attracts a bevy of beautiful women and that attracts a bevy of men who enjoy looking at beautiful women. Tuesdays are Karaoke time and Thursdays are College Nights. Once a week we run a promo party with one of our purveyors, from 8 to 10 p.m. Last night models from La Mas Agency were promoting Almendrado, an almond-flavored tequila that our customers really took to."

Dublin's is a big draw for college students of legal drinking age. "We cater to our college students with special prices from Monday through Friday. They have to show college ID and our staff carefully checks age ID at the same time," Johnson adds. "It's no coincidence that we're the number one West Coast account for Jack Daniels and Finlandia Vodka."

Opened in 1996, Dublin's has been so successful that a second unit opened in Irvine, California at the end of 1998.

WINE RACKS AT THE TABLES

"I am the pizza" was Sal Stellino's answer when asked why he put so much effort into each pizza he made in his small Italian ristorante in South Florida. That was 20 years ago. Now there are several Sal's Italian Ristorantes in Florida, three of them owned by Sam Purvis II, all of them run to Sal's exacting quality standards.

The Boynton Beach location has 11 booths and three tables. A wine rack holding six bottles is mounted on the wall, or partition, of every booth. A bottle of Chianti sits on each of the three tables. Eighteen wines from California and Italy are offered, priced from $13.95 to $34.95.

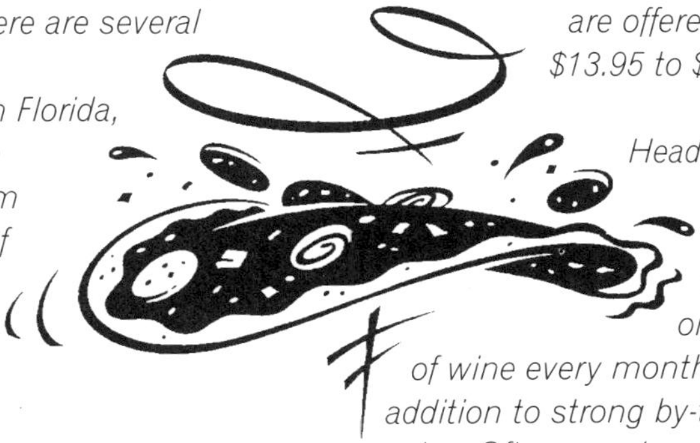

Head Server T. J. Mulroney says they consistently sell 200 or more bottles of wine every month. This is in addition to strong by-the-glass sales. Often guests select one of the wines in the wine rack at their booth.

For Beverage Industry Readers

Since 1992, Miro Anaya has represented many beverage clients for promotional events in restaurants and at trade shows. In 1999, she formed La Mas, The Maximum Services Agency, for promotional assignments not only in Southern California but in all major markets. She has personally trained over 58 female models, 25 male models and 15 gay market models, as of this writing.

When I was interviewing California restaurants for *Beverage Biz is Show Biz!,* I observed the professionalism and contagiously cheerful approach she and her staff brought to two introductory restaurant promotions for Almendrado Tequila, an excellent new almond-flavored tequila. She was also knowledgeable enough to introduce me to some of the restaurateurs featured in these pages.

You can telephone her at (310) 365-1106, fax (310) 798-2396*51 or write: La Mas, 2110-B Artesia Boulevard, Suite 316, Redondo Beach, CA 90278.

Let's Make A Daiquiri

That's not a bad idea and it's also the name of a unique concept that's flourishing on Pier 17 at New York's South Street Seaport as well as in New Orleans, Miami, Washington, D.C., and Hawaii.

"We take people back to a romantic time in the tropics when a daiquiri or a piña colada made them forget about everyday business cares and simply enjoy themselves and their companion," says bartender Raymond Rosa. "I've been at the South Street Seaport location since it opened in 1985, and one thing has been constant — everybody raves about our drinks. They ask why our daiquiris and coladas are so much better than those they get anyplace else and we just smile and shrug."

The secret is using fresh pineapple and pineapple juice in the pineapple piña coladas and daiquiris, a whole banana in the banana drinks and fresh strawberries and limes in the strawberry and lime drinks — that and a scoop of vanilla ice cream in each drink. Does it make a difference? 175,000 daiquiris and piña coladas a year at the Seaport says it does.

"Our customers tell us that when they can't afford a weekend in the tropics, they come in here. After a few sips they close their eyes and it feels as if they're on the beach in Tahiti," says manager Chris Fagan.

Index
— To Restaurants & Services —

The Alamo 65-69
New York, New York

Angelo and Maxie's 112-114
New York, New York

The Arches 157-158
Newport Beach, California

Ashes Steak House and Seafood Raw Bar 52-54
Red Bank, New Jersey

Babalu Lounge 111
Vancouver, British Columbia

The Balboa Bay Club 19-21
Newport Beach, California

Barmedia - Robert Plotkin 168-172
(800) 421-7179

Bern's Steak House 49-51
Tampa, Florida

Bryant & Cooper Steak House 44-45
Roslyn, New York

The Carltun 129-131
Havana
Palm Court
The Wine Cellar
East Meadow, New York

Cité 124-125
New York City, New York

Comfort Diners 175-176
New York, New York

Cooper's Classic Cars and Cigar Bar 179-180
New York City, New York

Cork's Steak House 163-164
Naples, Florida

Cowboy Palace Saloon 168
Chatsworth, California

Cozymel's Coastal Mexican Grill 85-88
El Segundo, California
and Westbury, New York

Dublin's Irish Whiskey Pub 182
West Hollywood, California

Dylan's 107-108
New York, New York

Extreme Bartending by Bar Smart 100-103
4869 Lanark Street
Vancouver, B.C., Canada, V5N 3S1
(604) 879-1036

Farfalla Trattoria and Wine Bar 138-140
Tinley Park, Illinois

Fiftyseven Fiftyseven 36-38
Four Seasons Hotel
New York, New York

Focaccia Grill 126-128
Wantagh, New York

Foghorn's Roadhouse 111
Vancouver, British Columbia

Fred's Uptown Tavern 111
Vancouver, British Columbia

Giovanni Ristorante 41-43
New York, New York

The Harvest 141-144
Pomfret, Connecticut

Heartbeat Restaurant 150
New York, New York

Hennessey's Tavern 89-90
Hermosa Beach, California

Hilton Chicago & Towers 31-33
Buckingham's
Kitty O'Shea's
Lakeside Green
Michigan Avenue Martini Bar
Pavilion Restaurant
Chicago, Illinois

Hotel Dakota 111
Vancouver, British Columbia

Il Cigno 154-156
Scarsdale, New York

The Irish Bank 92-94
San Francisco, California
and New York, New York

Jeff Ruby's 16-18
Cincinnati, Ohio

Laight Street 107-108
New York, New York

La Mas, The Maximum Service Agency 182-183
Redondo Beach, California

The Lamplighter 173-174
Rochester, New York

Layla 150-151
New York, New York

Let's Make A Daiquiri 184
New York, New York

The Lighthouse Cafe 91
Hermosa Beach, California

London Lennies 132-137
Rego Park, New York

Mai-Kai Restaurant and Show Room 26-30
Fort Lauderdale, Florida

McCormick & Schmick's . .34-35
El Segundo, California

Michi Restaurant & Bar 104-106
Manhattan Beach, California

Montrachet 146-149
New York, New York

Myriad Restaurant Group 146-153
New York, New York

The North Star Pub 70-75
New York, New York

Pizza Man 159-160
Milwaukee, Wisconsin

Poor Red's 180-181
El Dorado, California

Private Preserve 12, 123, 128, 159
P.O. Box 2841
Napa Valley, CA 94558
(707) 252-4258

The Queen Mary 46-48
Long Beach, California

The Roxy 109-111
Vancouver, British Columbia

Sal's Italian Ristorante 183
Boynton Beach, Florida

SideBern's 50-51
Tampa, Florida

SoHo Grand Hotel 63-64
New York, New York

Starwood Hotels 55-58

Southampton Publick House 76-80
Southampton, New York

Spenger's Seafood House 35
Berkeley, California

Terra 161-162
Naples, Florida

Tommy Bahama's Tropical Cafe 22-25
Naples, Florida

Tony's Off Third 161-162
Naples, Florida

Tribeca Grill 148
New York, New York

Tricks On Tap 115-117
325 Park Avenue
Mahtomedi, MN 55115
(800) Loudini

"21" Club 60-62
New York, New York

Vogue Theatre 111
Vancouver, British Columbia

The Waterfront 14-17
Coconut Joe's
Las Brisas
The South Beach Grill
Covington, Kentucky

Windows On The World 57, 120-123
New York, New York

Windows On The World Wine School 120-122
16 Woodstock Lane
New Paltz, New York 12561
(914) 255-1456

Wolfgang Puck Cafe 83-84
El Segundo, California
and Santa Monica, California

Index

— To People —

a

Jerry Alajajian 24
Felix Albano 36-38
Miro Anaya 34, 182-183
Brian Arbesfeld 118, 126-128
Mike Amidzich 145, 159-160

b

Colin Bannon 100-101
Joan Barnes 136
Leonard Barnes 136
Les Barnes 118, 132-137
Phil Barragato 81, 87-88
Joe Baum 122
John Belle 74
Rodrigo Bernal 130
Deven Black 59, 70-75
Susan Blank 38
Erik Blauberg 60-62
Mike Bolivar 30
Michael Bonadies 145, 147,
. 150-153
David Bouley 146
John Brecher 118
Adrian Bridge 54

c

Vance Campbell 100, 102,
. 109-111
Anthony Capetola 129
Kevin Carrigan 112-114
Walter Carrillo 82, 86-87
Nick Castronova 173-174
Ken Collura 49
Rory Connolly 81, 92
Peter Cooper 141-142
Sharon Cooper 119, 141-144
Blaine Culling 109-110
Elliot Cuker 179-180

d

Richard D'Amico 24
Gilles De Chambure 20
Dale DeGroff 95-99
Robert DeNiro 148
Steve DePietro 145, 154-156
Aubert de Villaine 50
Vince Didia 138
Blake Donaldson 95, 104-106
Veronique Drouhin 147

e

Doc Eason 115
Jean-Pierre Eigenheer 20
Bob Emfield 24

f

Chris Fagan 184
Joe Fassler 165-167
Giovanni Francescotti 41-43
Ira Freehof 165, 175-176
Barry Frommer 118, 133

g

Dorothy J. Gaiter 118
Troy Gallant 27
Mark Gambuzza 39, 52-53
Lucio Dalla Gasperina 24
Mike Gerber 89
Jimmy Gibson 16
David Gordon 148-149
Gary Gross 53

h

Paul Hennessey 90-91
Pedro Hernandez 65
Dan Hickey 75
Cyndi Holland 23-24
Sukie Honeycutt 161-162

ijk

Andrea Immer 39, 55-58

Daniel Johnnes 146-147,
. . . . .151, 153
Kat Johnson 182

Frank Klein 180-181

l

James Labe 150
Antonio Lara 69
Remi Lauvand 147
Bern Laxer 49
David Laxer 40, 49
Gert Laxer 49
Barbara Lazaroff 84
Dave Levy 30
Michael Lomanica 120
Len LoRusso 126-128

m

Jeff McBride 29
Mike McCann 124-125
Eddie McGhie 65
Andy MacBeth .101-102, 110-111
John Mantone 107
Dan Marcheano 145, 157-158
Tony Margolis 13, 23-25
John Mariani 154
Phil Markowski 78
Chris Martin 82, 92-94
Kern Mattei 27-29
Steve Matthews 90
Brian Matzkow 59, 63-64
Louis Melamed 115-117
Michi 105
Brian Miller 146
Mike Miller 32-33
Craig Mitchell 89
Robert Mondavi 158
Peter Mooney 44
T. J. Mulroney 183

n

Brent Nardi 139
Morris Nathanson 136
Drew Nieporent 145-148, 151
Tracy Nieporent 147-148
Judy Nissley 181

Cloyde Pate 163-164
Jim Pastorio 182
Robert Plotkin 165, 168-172
Sasha Poceckovic 101-102,
. 110-111
Gillis Poll 44-45
Nelson Portela 65-69
Wolfgang Puck 83-84
Sam Purvis II 183

Ruth Reichl 42
Edwin Rios 13, 31, 33
Dan Romelo 163
Raymond Rosa 184
Jeff Ruby 13-18
Pepe Ruiz 98
Bob Rustigian 168-169

Rhonda Sarnicola 168
Henry Schielein 13, 19, 21
Martin Shapiro 147
Christopher Shipley 62
Monte Silva 81, 83-84
Scott Smith 34-35
Tim Smith 47
Linda Sondik 113
Mike Speegle 181
Sal Stellino 183
Dave Stevens 16
Jack Streich 78
Larry Stone 147
Don Sullivan 59, 76-78, 80
Jim Sullivan 76
Kevin Sullivan 76-77, 80
Tom Symenski 33

Jack Thornton 30
Mireille Thornton 30
Robert Thornton 30
Gil Travalin 119, 129-130
John Tunney 129, 131

Neil Wallace 40, 46-48
Michael Waterhouse . .95, 107-108
Carole White 138-140

Scott Young 95, 100-103, 110

Natalie Zalevska 129
Kevin Zraly 119-123

Editor's Note

Restaurant Biz is Show Biz!

Why Marketing is *The* Key to Your Success

If you own or manage a restaurant now — or plan to one day open your own restaurant — you'll profit from reading *Restaurant Biz is Show Biz!* by Dave Steadman.

Written in Dave's clear, engaging style, the first eight chapters offer a blueprint for success, followed by 38 chapters that tap into the marketing tactics of successful restaurateurs, along with words of advice from industry pundits.

For your copy send $24 (plus sales tax for NY residents) to Spirited Living, 38 Broadway, Greenlawn, NY 11740. There is no charge for shipping and handling.

If you are reading a borrowed copy of *Beverage Biz Is Show Biz!* and would like a copy for yourself or a friend, send $36.00 (plus sales tax for NY residents) for each copy to Spirited Living, 38 Broadway, Greenlawn, NY 11740. There is no charge for shipping and handling.

Send payment by check or money order in U. S. funds only. For delivery to a foreign country, please add $12 U.S.